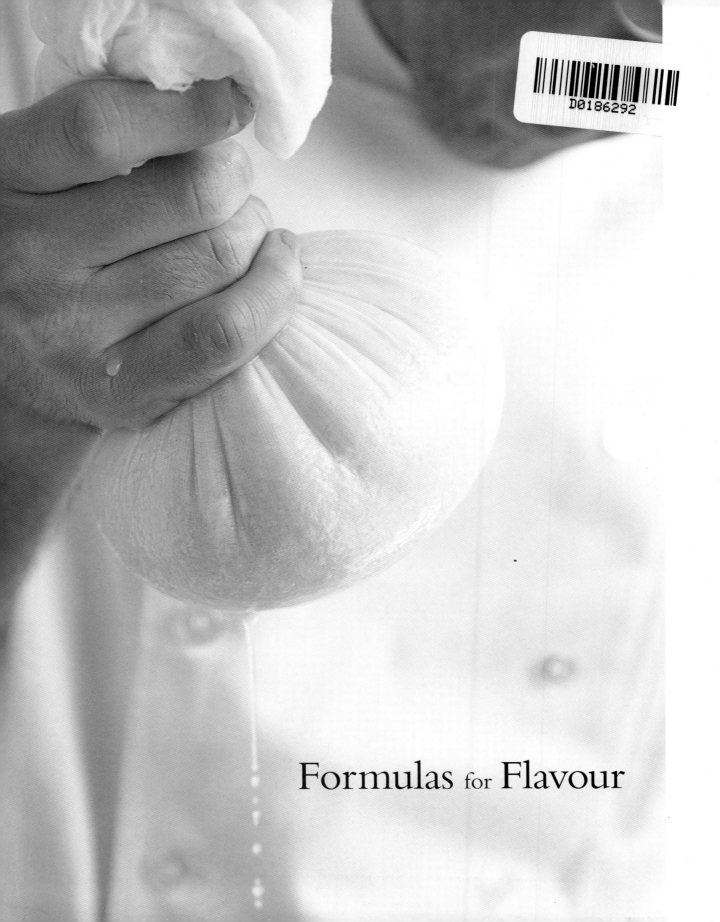

Formulas for Flavour

John Campbell

Foreword by **Heston Blumenthal**
Photography by **Sam Bailey**

Formulas for Flavour

How to cook
restaurant dishes
at home

Dedication

For my wife Gill and son Oliver, for their continued love and support.

First published in 2001 by Conran Octopus Limited, a part of Octopus Publishing Group,
a Hachette Livre Company, 2-4 Heron Quays, London E14 4JP
www.conran-octopus.co.uk
This paperback edition published in 2005, reprinted in 2006, 2007.

Publishing Director: Lorraine Dickey
Editorial Cookery Consultant: Jenni Muir
Senior Editor: Katey Day
Creative Director: Leslie Harrington
Art Editor: Carl Hodson
Production Director: Zoë Fawcett

The publishers would like to thank Jean Cazals, Claire Clifton and Christine Rickerby for their
work on this title.

British Cataloguing-in-Publication Data. A catalogue record for this book is available from the
British Library

ISBN 978 1 84091 429 0

Printed and bound in China

Contents

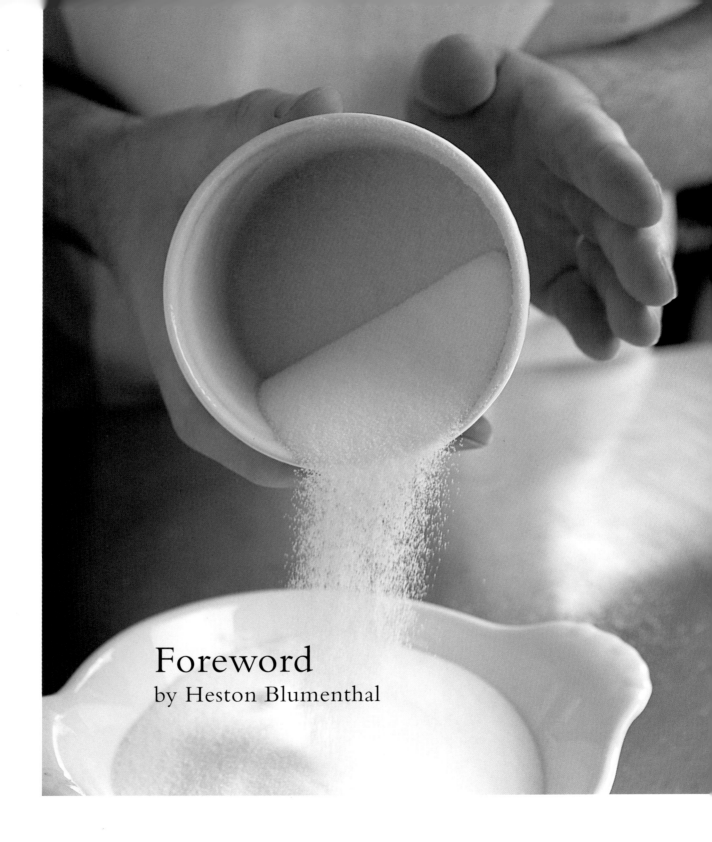

Foreword
by Heston Blumenthal

We are approaching a new era of gastronomy. An era that I believe will be the most exciting and challenging so far and one that I hope will cause chefs and domestic cooks alike to become inquisitive; being prepared to challenge, not for challenge's sake but for the desire to understand and improve.

The saying "We are what we eat" could also be re-phrased "We eat what we are". Our palates are so dominated by our preconceptions that, in many cases, we are unable to separate the two. Whether we try to recreate or eliminate childhood flavours depends on what we associate them with. Most of us will quite happily eat prawn cocktail but are disgusted at the thought of eating a grasshopper! In Britain we cherish the nursery-school comfort that rice pudding brings but the Japanese find the thought of eating sweet, creamed rice quite repellent.

Where does texture, taste and pre-conception merge? If we bite into a biscuit that is soft when it should not be, we pick up stale notes before we actually taste them. A fizzy drink that has become flat will taste sweeter and a soft, pappy apple will not taste fresh. The exploration and understanding of the link between our brain and palate is fascinating yet still in its infancy.

Cooking is about the only thing that we can do that involves all of the senses. If we see the colour red, nothing in our minds will question it; with food however, we have the use of sight, sound, smell taste and texture. These are all intrinsically linked. Couple this with the influence of the mind and it is easy to see why the most complex genetic map in the body is the one that links the brain to the palate.

All of this may seem too advanced, however it is a lot more approachable than many people think. Eating is something we all have to do to live, so why don't we think a little more about it?

I have known John for several years and have seen him grow enormously as a chef. He has three of the most important attributes a cook could hope to possess: honesty, integrity and taste. This combined with his tireless energy for improving and wonderful inquisitiveness place him firmly at the forefront of the new breed of British chef. While talking to John, it soon becomes evident that even with all of his achievements to date, he feels that he is only just beginning; the future for him and us is very exciting.

In this book, John has managed to provide the professional and amateur cook alike with a fantastic array of recipes and techniques that will not only be an asset in the kitchen but also a visual delight to people who are just interested in eating good food.

I really do believe that this book achieves a rare thing by offering valuable information to chefs while at the same time making the world of gastronomy approachable to all.

Cooking like a chef at home
HOW TO USE THIS BOOK

This book offers the next best thing to a day working in a professional kitchen, which would be a great learning experience for anyone interesting in cooking. The success of my dishes comes from adhering to traditional culinary logic but modernising the execution and sometimes introducing unexpected, but carefully considered, flavour combinations. I also like to include interesting contrasts of texture and temperature, both of which have an impact on the flavour.

Many of these recipes can be time consuming to produce but sometimes there is simply no shortcut to achieving a certain level of flavour. If you exercise patience and good planning on the more complex dishes, I think you will find the results are well worth it.

In writing this book I have tried to select recipes and describe them in such a way that gives an insight into the dynamics of either the dish, the ingredient, or the cooking method. The aim is to give you a clear overall understanding of the cooking process.

Once you have mastered the fundamental aspects of various dish components such as making pasta, soufflés, risottos, ice cream, dressings and sauces, or cooking meat and fish, you are then in a good position to create your own dishes. This could start simply by varying the ingredients to include your favourite flavourings or whatever is in season, and move on to breaking down the building blocks of my dishes and combining them in new ways. A good example: the roast plums served as a dessert with honey and yogurt ice cream (page 106), can be cooked a little longer to serve with roast venison (page 101) and accompanied by fondant potatoes or wild mushroom risotto (pages 93 and 73), some braised shallots (page 160) and red wine jus (page 163). Or the plums could be served with muesli for breakfast.

There are a great many variables involved in cooking: individual oven temperatures differ, some ingredients cook more quickly than others, the temperatures at which they are combined can effect the end result, the list is endless. My aim here is not to eliminate the risks entirely, but to identify the potential pitfalls. The step-by-step photography will help to clarify the key stages of each dish and, in the Science and Methodology section, certain risk areas are explained to help you avoid them.

Home cooks do not have the resources of a professional kitchen or 8-10 chefs working along side them but first-class results are possible when you prepare certain parts of the dish

in advance. In a restaurant this is known by the French term mis-en-place, which means having everything in place or prepared beforehand. It is just as important in the home kitchen, especially when cooking for guests, to have as much as possible made in advance, ready and within reach at the time of service. However, there are some elements of a dish that simply cannot be completed in advance without detriment to the final result. The Thinking Ahead section at the beginning of each starter, main course and dessert recipe clarifies your options here.

The added benefits of thorough planning and advance preparation are that they will help you enjoy a more relaxed, controlled and pleasurable environment at the point of serving, and thus build confidence in the kitchen, which is perhaps the most important ingredient of all. You will then be well on the way to developing your own signature dishes.

INGREDIENTS Some ingredients may be more difficult to source than others, but you should be able to find most of them. The relationships you have with your butcher and fishmonger are paramount, as meat and fish are the centre-pieces of so many meals. Try to avoid supermarket chains when buying these ingredients; the smaller specialized outlets should be able to source a wider range of ingredients and supply them to your specifications. They will also carry out much preparation work if you have a good relationship.

SEASONING The old myth that including salt and pepper pots in a table setting is disrespectful to the chef is nonsense. We all have different tastes, some have a low tolerance to sodium and others a high tolerance. It is hard to achieve a fine balance between the two, but so important to the final product. The aim is not to taste the salt but to use the salt to enhance the flavour of the main ingredient. Some good rules to follow when seasoning:

• Use fine flakes of naturally produced salt as less are needed
• When tasting to check the seasoning, bear in mind you are only tasting a spoonful. It may taste fine in small amounts but could be over-salted if you were to eat the whole dish
• Remember that you can always add salt but not take it away
• Correct the seasoning at serving temperature. The optimum temperature range at which taste buds are most active is 20-40°C/68-104°F , with sweetness emphasized at the lower end of that range and salty/bitter at the higher end.

KITCHEN APPLIANCES Domestic appliances tend to be less powerful than the industrial appliances used in professional kitchens, however the calibre of domestic models also varies. When making purées, ice creams, soups and so on at home, a little adjustment may be needed. Be careful not to overheat any motor driven appliances. If they get too hot just stop, allow them to cool and, once cool, resume the task.

INSTINCTS This book shows how many traditional cooking techniques work and how they can be applied to modern dishes. Rather than being confining, a good understanding of techniques frees you from being too dependent on following directions parrot fashion. People who have a thorough grasp of the basic nature of food and its key cooking methods are in a better position to correct any inadvertent mistakes and develop a more spontaneous and free-flowing way of working in the kitchen.

Planning your cooking

Home cooks do not have the same resources as a professional kitchen, so when finishing a restaurant-style dish there will invariably be more than one or two components to deal with, which can seem stressful. The list below offers ways to keep things prepared earlier warm and ready to serve, helping you to feel more in control of the serving process.

- Decide first where you will lay out the serving plates.
- If you have a microwave oven, use it. Usually the sauce can be made in advance and placed in a container in the fridge, then reheated at the last moment. The same is true of most vegetable garnishes, as long as the basic principles were adhered to when preparing and cooking them beforehand the end result will not be affected. Remember when reheating food in a microwave oven to create an opening for the steam to escape.
- If the recipe demands using your main oven at the last moment before serving, heat the serving plates earlier and then remove and wrap them in foil to retain the heat.
- Ask yourself whether you can put one element of the dish on the table in a serving dish. This will relieve some pressure and free essential stove space.
- Try to clean up as you go, otherwise, before you know it, the sink will be piled high with dishes and the work surfaces covered with pots and pans. Keep your space clear and it will make a big difference.

- Once things are hot and you are nearing service, place each item in an ovenproof dish, cover with foil and place in the oven on a very low setting (60–70°C/140–160°F). The garnish will hold at serving temperature for a while, giving you time to finish cooking the fish or meat and still serve everything hot at the same time.

Planning a dinner party

Do not go overboard trying to impress guests as it makes them and you feel uncomfortable. It is more important to be calm and organized, and you achieve this by being fully aware of your resources and preparing as much of the meal in advance as possible without jeopardizing the end result.

When selecting a menu, aim for one 'wow' dish and two that are simple but effective. A good example would be to choose a starter that is made and plated in advance or simply requires a brief reheat, such as pea soup with tortellini of ham hock (page 18). The main course could be more difficult, perhaps a dish with an element of surprise such as slow-cooked beef with onion ice cream (page 88). Then dessert would best be something that was prepared in advance and simply needs baking, such as chocolate and griottine clafoutis (page 110).

Watch the portion sizes when serving a three course menu. Most people do not eat three-course meals everyday and it would be a shame to spend a great deal of time and energy on a terrific dessert and then have guests unable to finish it.

If you are not sure about a certain element of a dish, try it out the week before on close friends or family; on special occasions it is best to serve something you have cooked before and are comfortable with. Also consider how you will transfer the food from the kitchen to the table (and remember that if the dining table is in the kitchen, it is even more important to look organized, especially if the occasion is relatively formal).

Other key considerations when planning a dinner party are the time of year – seasonal produce will be far superior – and any special dietary requirement of your guests. I find that, even when you enquire in advance, there is often one person at a dinner party who cannot or will not eat something and this does not become apparent until they are sitting awkwardly at the table. I always have something extra prepared such as roast artichokes or mushroom risotto (pages 23 and 73) that can be easily pulled from the fridge if necessary. This degree of forward planning may seem overly conscientious but it will help make your evening a complete success.

Starters

Roast Salt Cod and Clam Chowder

I tend to be bored by plain soups. There is only so much you can do with them by themselves, so I add another dimension by introducing a secondary ingredient. In the case of this great, hearty soup it is salt cod, and in the following pea soup recipe it is tortellini. Try it yourself when making other soups, especially for dinner parties. If you want to skip salting the cod, the dish will still work, but salting firms up the texture, eliminating the fish's naturally flaky properties. SERVES 4

SALT COD
400g/14oz cod fillet, skinned and trimmed
200g/7oz/¾ cup sea salt
2 tbsp ground cumin
1 tbsp five-spice powder

CLAMS
500g/1lb2oz Manilla or Venus clams, shells tightly closed

2 medium shallots, finely diced
50g/2oz/½ stick butter
200ml/7floz/scant 1 cup white wine or vermouth

CHOWDER
50ml/2floz/¼ cup corn oil
50g/2oz smoked bacon, cut into 1cm/½in cubes
1 medium onion, cut into 1cm/½in dice

1 medium carrot, cut into 1cm/½in dice
2 cloves garlic, finely chopped
1 stick celery, cut into 1cm/½in dice
1 medium yellow bell pepper, cut into 1cm/½in dice
1 medium potato, peeled and cut into 1cm/½in dice
1 litre/1¾ pints/4½ cups fish stock (see page 157)

100ml/4floz/½ cup cream
50g/2oz/ ½ stick butter
salt and pepper

TO FINISH
50g/2oz/½ stick butter
1 head escarole leaves, picked over and ribs removed, or 200g/7oz spinach
50ml/2floz/¼ cup herb oil (see page 161)
chopped chervil

Thinking ahead The cod will need to be salted the day before, wrapped tightly in plastic and stored in the fridge. The fish stock and herb oil should also be made in advance. You will need to source the clams from a fishmonger but avoid buying on Mondays. The clams can be cooked a day in advance In fact, you could make the entire chowder the day before, which would make things much easier on the day of a dinner party.

FOR THE SALT COD Place the skinned and trimmed cod fillet on a tray. Rub the fish with the spices and sprinkle the salt evenly over the top; if the fish tapers at one end, reduce the amount of salt placed on this area, or it will over-cure. Wrap in plastic wrap and place in the fridge. After 1 hour, turn the cod fillet over and return to the fridge for another hour.

Fill a clean sink half-full with cold water. Unwrap the cod and rinse off the salt in the sink (1). Drain the water away and fill the sink halfway again. Leave the cod to soak for 30 minutes. Remove from the water, dry well and wrap tightly in a new piece of plastic. Place in the fridge overnight.

FOR THE CLAMS Take a large saucepan with a tight-fitting lid and place over a medium heat with the shallots and butter. Cook for 1 minute without letting the shallots brown.

Add the washed clams, shake the pan, then add the wine and place the lid on the pan immediately. Leave the clams to steam for 1–2 minutes so that they open and exude an intense liquor.

Remove the lid and make sure all the clams are open (2); if only 95 percent are open, remove the pan from the heat and discard any with closed shells. Place a colander over a large bowl, and pour the contents of the pan into the colander, reserving the liquor for the chowder. Allow the clams to cool.

Pick out the meat (3) and discard the shells. Store the clam meat in an airtight container in the fridge until you are ready to serve the chowder.

FOR THE CHOWDER In a large saucepan, heat the oil. Add the bacon and cook for about 5 minutes until crisp and brown. Using a perforated spoon, remove the bacon to some paper towel to drain.

Add the onion, carrot, garlic and celery to the saucepan, reduce the heat to medium-low and cook the vegetables for 2–3 minutes without letting them colour. Add the bell peppers and potatoes and cook for 5 minutes, again without colouring.

Pour in the reserved liquor from the clams and the fish stock. Bring to a boil and simmer for 10 minutes or until the volume of liquid has reduced by half.

Add the cooked bacon and cream (4), then bring to the boil and reduce for a further 2 minutes until the soup thickens slightly. At this point the soup can be cooled and stored for 2 days in a covered container in the fridge, but is best made on the day of serving.

TO COMPLETE Remove the cod fillet from the fridge and cut it into 4 equal portions. If the soup has been chilled, place it in a saucepan and heat through slowly over a low heat. Whisk in the butter to finish.

Meanwhile, in a large pan, melt 50g/2oz/½ stick of butter over a high heat. Add the escarole, or spinach, and leave to wilt (5). Drain and set aside, keeping it warm.

Heat a non-stick frying pan on the stove with 50ml/2floz/¼ cup corn oil. Add the cod portions and cook for 2 minutes until golden brown on one side (6). Turn and remove the pan from the heat, allowing the cod to finish cooking off the stove in the residual heat of the pan.

Add the clams to the hot chowder and stir for 30 seconds until they are reheated. Place the escarole in a small ball in the centre of the serving bowls. Lay the cod on top of this. Spoon in the chowder (7), then the herb oil. Garnish with chervil and serve.

Soup of Pea, Tortellini of Ham Hock

This is a great combination of popular flavours – pea and ham, pea and mint. A real winter dish, it can be served as a simple yet effective starter for a dinner party, or as a hearty main course if you make the tortellini a little bigger and serve the soup with some warm crusty bread. Frozen peas are a good substitute for fresh when out of season and will help simplify the preparation of this recipe. **SERVES 6**

HAM HOCK
1 ham hock, soaked
  overnight
1 carrot, peeled
½ onion, peeled
1 bay leaf
1 clove garlic

TORTELLINI
200g/7oz chicken mousse
  (see page 159)
2 tsp chopped chives
1 batch pasta dough
  (see page 159)

SOUP
1kg/2lb4oz fresh or
  frozen peas
2 tsp corn oil
2 shallots, chopped
500ml/18floz/2¼ cups milk
100ml/4floz/½ cup double
  (heavy) cream
100g/4oz/1 stick butter

TO FINISH
50ml/2floz/¼ cup mint oil
  (see page 162)
sprigs of chervil

Thinking ahead You need to start the ham hock at least 3 days before serving. The first job is to soak the ham overnight to remove any excess salt. Cook it the next day, strip the meat from the bone and store it covered in the fridge, All the other main components of this dish can be made up to 6 hours before serving. If you really want to save time on the day of a dinner party, the soup, tortellinis and mint oil could all be made in advance and frozen – the soup and mint oil for 1 month, the tortellinis for 1 week. When freezing the soup, freeze only the liquidized soup base and whisk in the cream and butter just as you are reheating the soup ready for serving.

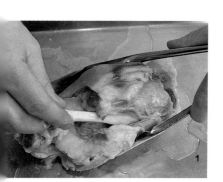

FOR THE HAM HOCK Soak the ham hock overnight to remove excess salt. Next day, remove the hock from the soaking water and wash well.

Place the hock in a stockpot with the carrot, onion, bay and garlic, then cover with water. Bring to a boil and simmer for 4 hours or until the pin bone can be removed easily leaving no meat attached (1). Allow the ham hock to cool in the cooking liquor.

When cool, remove and peel away all the fat, bone and sinew, leaving lean meat (2). Cut into 5mm/¼in dice and store in the fridge until ready for use.

FOR THE TORTELLINI MOUSSE Place the chicken mousse in a bowl. Add the chives and diced ham hock and fold in carefully, taking care not to overwork the mixture, which will cause it to separate (see page 166).

FOR THE TORTELLINI Place a large saucepan on the stove and bring to the boil. Using a rolling pin, roll out the pasta dough to 2mm/⅛in thick then, using a pastry cutter, cut it into discs approximately 5cm/2in wide (3).

Using a pasta machine, roll out each pasta disc to a 13cm/5in round, turning the pasta 180 degrees through each turn (4). Lay the rounds on a lightly floured surface.

Place a heaped teaspoon of mousse on each pasta disc (5). Fold over the top of the pasta and seal both sides with water to give a half-circle. Use a cutter to help pack the filling neatly (6), then trim off the joined ends, leaving at least 2.5cm/1in pasta around the mousse.

Place the pasta parcel in front of you with the curved side facing away from you. Holding each end with the forefinger and thumb of each hand (7), press the ends together firmly, creating a solid join (8). At this point the tortellini could be placed on a floured tray, covered and frozen for 1 week.

Fill a large bowl with cold water and a few ice cubes ready to refresh the pasta after cooking. Place the tortellini in the boiling water, cook for 3 minutes, then remove and refresh in the icy water. At this point the tortellini could be drizzled with a little oil and stored in a covered container in the fridge until ready to serve.

FOR THE SOUP Blanch the peas in a small saucepan of boiling water for 2–3 minutes, then drain.

Heat the oil in large saucepan and cook the shallots for 2–3 minutes without letting them brown. Add the peas and cook for a further 2–3 minutes, again without colouring. Pour in the milk, bring to a simmer and cook until the peas are tender.

Cool the mixture slightly, then transfer it to a food processor and blend until very smooth – this may take a while. At this point, the soup can be left to cool completely, then stored in an airtight container in the fridge until ready to serve.

TO COMPLETE Place the soup in a clean pan, add the cream and butter and bring to a simmer, whisking until the butter is well incorporated. Reheat the tortellini in a pan of boiling water for 2–3 minutes (5–6 minutes if frozen), then drain and place in the bottom of some warm soup bowls. Pour in the soup, drizzle with mint oil, garnish with chervil sprigs and serve.

Chef's notes For a vegetarian dish, the tortellini could be replaced with a deep-fried pea fritter made using some tempura batter (see page 163) and around 25g/1oz/¼ cup peas per portion. Simply stir the peas into the batter at a ratio of 90 per cent peas to 10 per cent batter. Fry tablespoons of the mixture in corn oil until golden brown on both sides.

5

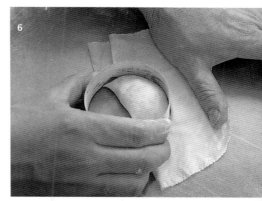

6

7

8

Roast Artichoke, Ratatouille, Olive and Basil Dressing

Always a winner with those who do not eat meat, this uncomplicated dish has a warm Mediterranean feel. It is the dish I always have prepared in reserve for dinner parties when someone unexpectedly reveals they are vegetarian or avoiding a particular food. In those situations, guests are hugely impressed when you can quickly pull out a dish like this. **SERVES 4**

ARTICHOKES

4 large globe artichokes, cooked as on page 38, choke removed
50ml/2floz/¼ cup olive oil
12 cloves garlic, unpeeled
2 sprigs thyme
sea salt
ground black pepper

RATATOUILLE AND BASIL DRESSING

80ml/3floz/⅓ cup olive oil
1 medium onion, finely diced
1 red bell pepper, cut into 1cm/½in dice
1 green bell pepper, cut into 1cm/½in dice
1 yellow bell pepper, cut into 1cm/½in dice
1 courgette (zucchini), cut into 1cm/½in dice
½ aubergine (eggplant), cut into 1cm/½in dice
1 tbsp tomato paste
500ml/18floz/2¼ cups tomato juice
500ml/18floz/2¼ cups vegetable nage (see page 158)
2 tbsp green olive tapenade (see page 160)

TO FINISH

150g/5oz extra fine green beans
1 batch aubergine caviar (see page 159)
a few chervil sprigs
a few chive tips
a little basil oil (see page 162)
4 savoury tuiles (see page 164)

Thinking ahead Preparing and cooking the artichokes the day before will save a great deal of time. The vegetable nage can be made 2 days before, while the basil oil and aubergine caviar can be made 1 day before. The tapenade lasts for 3 months chilled.

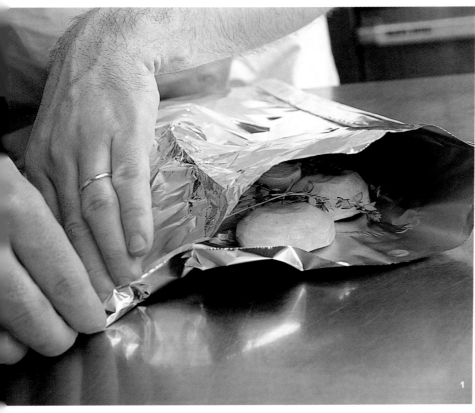

FOR THE ARTICHOKES Preheat the oven to 180°C/350°F/Gas 4. On a work surface, place a piece of foil large enough to contain the cooked globe artichokes. Place them on the foil with the oil, garlic, thyme, salt and pepper and fold over to make a package (1). Seal well, place on a baking sheet and cook in the oven for 15 minutes.

Remove from the oven, open the parcel, then return to the oven and continue cooking for 10 minutes. To test for doneness, pinch the garlic with your forefinger and thumb to ensure it is soft (2). Reseal the bag to keep the artichokes warm and set aside.

FOR THE RATATOUILLE AND BASIL DRESSING In a large saucepan, heat 2 tablespoons of the olive oil over a moderate heat. Add all the ratatouille vegetables and cook for 2 minutes without letting them colour.

Stir in the tomato paste and cook for a further 2 minutes. Pour in the tomato juice (3) and nage, bring to the boil

and simmer for 10–15 minutes or until reduced by half. Season with salt and pepper and keep warm.

TO COMPLETE Place a pan of salted water on the stove. Bring to a boil, add the green beans and simmer for 6–7 minutes until just cooked.

Meanwhile, in a small saucepan, heat the aubergine caviar through gently, stirring constantly to prevent burning.

Drain the beans, season to taste and divide them between the serving bowls. Top with the warm artichokes. Fill the artichoke with the aubergine caviar (4).

Divide the herbs between the serving bowls. Whisk the tapenade into the ratatouille mixture and pour it into the bowls (5). Garnish each dish with the basil oil, tuile and herbs, then serve.

Chef's notes The ratatouille can be paired with the roast lamb on page 92 and topped with a quenelle of aubergine caviar. Or simply toss it with pasta.

5

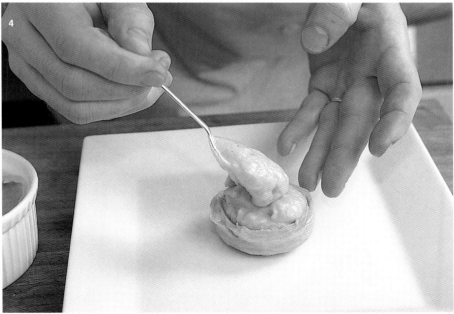

4

'Cheese, Tomato and Onion'
(Goats' Cheese Ravioli with Tomato Fondu and Pickled Onions)

The Italian combination of tomato and basil finds its way onto most menus in some form or another, and why not? It works well and the flavours are fresh and clean. This dish includes cheese in the form of a light ravioli that complements the tomato and basil. Pickled onions provide an extra taste dimension. They are not often seen on fine dining menus but their sweet, sour and spicy flavours are excellent in this context. SERVES 6

PICKLED ONIONS
30 small pickling or baby
  onions, peeled and
  trimmed
300ml/11floz/1½ cups
  white wine vinegar
90g/3½oz/1⅓ cups sugar
1 red chilli, deseeded and
  chopped
1 tsp Chinese five-spice
  powder
½ stick cinnamon
1 tsp finely chopped
  pickled ginger

RAVIOLI
100g/3½ strongly flavoured
  soft goats' cheese such as
  Capricorn or chèvre log
75g/3oz/¾ cup strongly
  flavoured Cheddar cheese,
  grated
1 tsp snipped chives
300g/10½oz chicken
  mousse (see page 159)
100g/3½oz pasta dough
  (see page 159)
salt and pepper

FONDU
8 ripe plum tomatoes (plus
  the trimmings from the
  tomato and basil dressing)
50ml/2floz/¼ cup olive oil
1 large shallot, finely
  chopped
½ tsp chopped coriander
  (cilantro)

TOMATO AND
BASIL DRESSING
3 plum tomatoes
3 fresh basil leaves

100ml/4floz/½ cup olive oil
50ml/2floz/¼ cup balsamic
  vinegar

BASIL FOAM
200ml/7floz/scant 1 cup
  milk
30 basil leaves

TO FINISH
250g/9oz mixed baby salad
  leaves
50ml/2floz/¼ cup basic
  vinaigrette (see page 162)

Thinking ahead The onions must be pickled at least 24 hours before serving to achieve the right balance between soft and crunchy. The chicken mousse can be made 1 or 2 days in advance, but do not combine it with the cheese. The pasta could be made the day before. The tomato and basil dressing and basil foam both need to be completed just before serving.

FOR THE PICKLED ONIONS

Place all the ingredients in a medium saucepan and bring to a boil. Remove from the heat and place an airtight container (this is important as the odour could make the fridge smell).

Take a piece of plastic wrap, lay it over the onions and push down on them to expel the air. Ensure the top layer is covered with pickling juices and place in the fridge for 24 hours to cure.

FOR THE RAVIOLI
Place both cheeses and the chives in a mixing bowl and mix well until the goats' cheese has softened. Fold in the chicken mousse, being careful not to overwork the mixture as this will split the mousse (1). Chill for at least 2 hours.

Using a rolling pin, roll out the pasta dough to 2mm/⅛in thick then, using a pastry cutter, cut it into discs 5cm/2in wide (2). Cover to prevent drying.

Working with 2 pasta discs to complete a ravioli at a time, use a pasta machine to roll out each disc to a 13cm/5in round, turning the pasta 180 degrees through each turn. Lay the rounds on a lightly floured surface.

Fill a disposable piping bag with the cheese mixture. On one of the pasta discs, pipe the mousse in a mound 5cm/2in wide and 2.5cm/1in high (3). Lay the other pasta disc over the mousse (4) and seal the edges, ensuring all the air is expelled (5).

Use a cutter to help pack the filling neatly (6), then trim off the joined ends, leaving at least 2.5cm/1in pasta around the mousse. Place on a lightly floured tray and cover with plastic (7). Once the raviolis are made they will last 30-40 minutes before they will start to dry out and crack.

FOR THE FONDU Fill a saucepan large enough to accommodate 4 of the plum tomatoes with water and bring to the boil. Meanwhile, half-fill a bowl with water and ice to arrest the cooking. Core the 8 tomatoes for the fondu as well as the 3 tomatoes for the tomato and basil dressing, and score a cross at the rounded end of each.

When the water is boiling, carefully place 4 of the tomatoes in the pan and leave for just 8-10 seconds. Remove the tomatoes immediately and plunge into the iced water. Repeat twice with the remaining tomatoes.

Cut each tomato in quarters lengthways and remove the seeds (8). Lay on paper towel for 30 minutes to dry off the excess moisture.

When the tomatoes are dry, take 32 of the tomato quarters and roughly chop the flesh into 1cm/½in dice. Trim the remaining 12 tomato quarters into square fillets. Set aside the fillets to use in the dressing and roughly chop the trimmings to add to the fondu.

In a medium saucepan, heat the oil and cook the chopped shallot for 4 minutes without letting them brown. Add the diced tomatoes and cook for a further 1 minute until they just soften but still have a little structure left in the flesh. Remove from the heat, stir in the coriander and season to taste.

Spoon the fondu into a piece of muslin and set aside for 15-30 minutes so that the excess juice bleeds out (9).

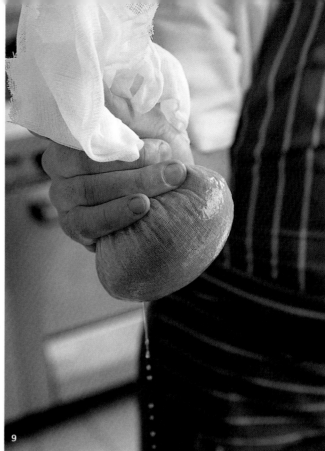

FOR THE BASIL FOAM In a small saucepan of boiling water, blanch the basil for 10 seconds, then drain.

Place the basil and milk in a food processor and liquidize. Strain the mixture into a medium saucepan and set aside until the completion stage.

FOR THE TOMATO AND BASIL DRESSING Dice the reserved squares of tomato fillet into 1cm/½in cubes. Have ready to hand the basil leaves, oil and balsamic vinegar as this dressing must be completed at the very last minute before serving.

TO COMPLETE Place a large pan of water on the stove with a scant handful of salt and bring to a gentle simmer.

Meanwhile, slowly warm the basil milk. Use a whisk or electric hand blender to agitate the milk to a foam resembling cappuccino froth. Set aside until ready to garnish the dish.

Place a pastry cutter or mould ring 6cm/2½in wide on one of the serving plates. Place 5 of the pickled onions in the ring towards the edge and spoon a layer of fondu (10) about 1cm/½in thick on top of this. Ensure a firm fit, then remove the ring (11). Repeat with the remaining serving plates.

Carefully place the raviolis into the simmering water and cook them for 7–8 minutes until firm.

Meanwhile, dress the salad leaves by placing them in a large bowl with the basic vinaigrette and tossing until the leaves are evenly coated. Place some of the dressed salad on top of the tomato fondu on each serving plate.

When the raviolis are cooked, remove them carefully from the water and lay them on a clean towel or some kitchen paper to drain briefly.

Finish the tomato and basil dressing by shredding the basil leaves finely and mixing them with the oil, balsamic vinegar and diced tomato. Drizzle the mixture evenly around each plate.

Place the raviolis on top of the salad. Quickly reagitate the basil foam if necessary and spoon the bubbles onto each serving to finish (12).

Chef's notes

The individual components of this dish are highly versatile and work well with other dishes in this book. For example, you could make the ravioli a little smaller and serve them with a piece of roast fish and a light sauce such as fennel cream (see page 65).

Risotto of Crab, Avocado Ice Cream

Crab and avocado go hand in hand and usually appear together on restaurant menus; this dish offers a modern twist on this classic combination. Risotto tends to be labeled as 'difficult' but the recipe below will help you understand the process and avoid potential pitfalls. Following the simple basic steps will help you achieve a perfect result every time. Give the risotto your full attention and stir continuously. The emulsion of stock and butter will determine how it will sit on the plate. A glutinous mound resembling savoury rice pudding is to be avoided, while a mass that just holds its own weight and is free from an excess of butter or stock is the ideal. **SERVES 6**

AVOCADO ICE CREAM
100g/4oz/½ cup sugar
85ml/3½floz/7 tbsp medium white wine
60g/2½oz/⅓ cup liquid glucose
75ml/3floz/⅓ cup water
2 ripe haas avocados
juice of 1 lemon
75ml/3floz/⅓ cup milk

RISOTTO BASE
1 litre/1¾ pints/4⅓ cups shellfish nage (see page 157)
50ml/2floz/¼ cup corn oil
2 shallots, finely chopped
½ clove garlic, halved
200g/7oz/1 cup carnaroli or arborio rice
4 tbsp white wine

SHELLFISH SAUCE
250ml/9floz/1 cup shellfish nage (see page 157)
250ml/9floz/1 cup semi-skimmed (half-fat) milk
50g/2oz/½ stick butter
salt and pepper

TO FINISH
100g/4oz fresh white crab meat, picked over
35g/1½oz/⅓ cup Parmesan cheese, grated
30g/1oz/¼ stick butter
2 tsp chopped chives
2 tbsp tomato concasse (see page 161)
sprigs of chervil

Thinking ahead The nage used in the risotto base and shellfish sauce can be made up to 1 month in advance if stored in the freezer and 3 days ahead if stored chilled. The ice cream can be made up to 2 days in advance. The tomato concasse can be prepared the day before serving while the risotto base can only be made 6-8 hours ahead. Before completion of the dish, make time to pick over the fresh crab meat carefully to ensure that no pieces of shell are inadvertently added to the risotto.

FOR THE ICE CREAM
In a small saucepan, dissolve the sugar, white wine, glucose and water over a low heat, then set aside to cool.

Transfer the mixture to a food processor, add the avocados and lemon juice and purée until very smooth (1). Mix in the milk.

Churn the mixture in an ice cream machine until frozen and store in the freezer. The ice cream should be made a minimum of 2 hours before serving to achieve full setting texture but will last frozen for up to 2 days.

FOR THE RISOTTO BASE
Bring the shellfish nage to a simmer in a saucepan. Heat the corn oil in a deep heavy saucepan over medium heat. Add the shallots and garlic then sweat for 3 minutes without letting them brown. Add the rice and sweat for a further

2 minutes, again without colouring. Pour in the wine and simmer until it has reduced to a glaze.

Add the hot nage in small batches of 50-75ml/2-3floz/¼-⅓ cup (2), bringing it to the boil each time and allowing it to evaporate while stirring the rice continuously. Each stage should take about 3 minutes. Repeat until the rice is nearly cooked but not chalky – the process will take about 14 minutes from the first addition of stock. Retain the excess nage for use when finishing.

Remove the risotto from the pan, ensuring that the rice is reasonably dry, and spread it over a tray (3). Set aside to cool, then store the risotto base in the fridge for up to 8 hours before serving.

FOR THE SHELLFISH SAUCE
Place the nage in a saucepan, bring to the boil and simmer until it is thick,

syrupy and about 50ml/2floz/¼ cup in volume (4). When you are almost ready to start plating the dish, add the butter and milk and use a whisk to mix well. The temperature of this sauce is important: it should be hot but not steaming. Do not let it boil.

TO COMPLETE
Remove the avocado ice cream from the freezer so that it may soften before serving.

Put the nage on the stove and heat it to simmering point. Have the shellfish sauce ready with warm serving plates waiting because just 2-3 minutes extra in the pan is the difference between a good and bad risotto.

Place a heavy, deep saucepan on the stove over a medium heat. Add the risotto, some of the hot nage and the butter and bring the mixture to a boil. Note that the quantity of nage given is approximate and the entire amount should only be added if the risotto becomes dry or thick. Cook the risotto for 2-3 minutes, stirring constantly, until the rice is tender and there is a smooth emulsion of stock and butter; the mass should just hold its own weight (5).

(If you are making risotto in the traditional fashion, begin here.) Add the crab, Parmesan cheese, tomato concasse and chives and fold together (6). Remember that the crab is already cooked and further cooking will cause it to become dry and tasteless.

Adjust the seasoning to taste and place the risotto in the centre of each serving plate. Using a whisk or electric hand blender, agitate the sauce until a cappuccino-like foam appears (7), then spoon the sauce around the risotto. Top each dish with a scoop of the avocado ice cream and some chervil, then serve.

Chef's notes

If you would prefer to use the traditional method of making risotto, increase the volume of stock by 200ml/7floz/scant 1 cup and cook the rice for a further 3-4 minutes. When the rice is done, add a splash of nage and the butter to start building the emulsion. You can then pick up the recipe from the point at which the crab, cheese and so on are stirred in. Always aim for a balance of stock and butter to give a perfect emulsion.

Roast Scallop with Artichoke Barigoule

I prefer hand-gathered scallops for my dishes. They cost a little more but the extra expense is worth it. Dredged scallops are, in my opinion, a little cruel. Large chain nets are dragged along the bottom of the scallop beds and the shells fill up with sand, silt, grit and mud and are battered around, stressing the scallop so that it shrinks — not very good at all. Nor do I like scallops soaked in a phosphate solution to preserve them. The scallop draws in the moisture from the solution, making it plumper and heavier. This means you are paying for water, and when the scallop hits the hot pan, a milky substance leaks out which causes the scallop to steam rather than sear. **SERVES 4**

SCALLOPS
4 extra large, 8 large or
  12 medium scallops

**ARTICHOKE
BARIGOULE**
4 medium globe artichokes
1 lemon
100ml/4floz/½ cup corn oil
1 large carrot, sliced
1 large onion, sliced
2 cloves garlic, crushed

50g/2oz/¼ cup mustard
  seeds
1 sprig thyme
1 bay leaf
50ml/2floz/¼ cup white
  wine
300ml/12floz/1½ cups
  chicken stock (see page
  157)

SAUCE D'ÉPICE
25ml/1floz/1½ tbsp corn oil
1 large carrot, chopped

1 small onion, chopped
1 tsp ground cumin
1 tsp five-spice powder
1 tsp medium curry powder
1 star anise
6 cloves
100ml/4floz/½ cup white
  wine
100ml/4floz/½ cup chicken
  stock (see page 157)
50ml/2floz/¼ cup double
  (heavy) cream
50g/2oz/¼ stick butter

GARNISH
50g/2oz/½ stick butter
2 large parsnips, peeled and
  cut into 16 x 2.5cm/1in
  batons
½ head escarole or cos
  lettuce
8 confit button onions
  (see page 160)
200g/7oz foie gras
  (optional)
4 slices black truffle
  (optional)

Thinking ahead The artichokes, can be prepared up to 4 days prior to serving, and the confit onions up to 2 days prior. The sauce d'épice and onions can be prepared a day in advance and reheated just before serving. Order your scallops well in advance from the fishmonger; in Britain, Wednesday to Friday are good days as this is when the transport comes down from Scotland where the scallops are caught.

FOR THE ARTICHOKES To trim the artichokes, cut away all the woody leaves and use a paring knife to round off any sharp edges (1-4). Rub the artichokes with a cut lemon every so often to prevent discoloration.

In a large saucepan of approximately 3 litre/5 pint/3½ quart capacity, heat the corn oil over a medium heat. Add the sliced carrot, onion, garlic, mustard seeds, thyme and bay leaf to the oil and cook for 3-4 minutes without letting them colour. Add the artichokes to the pan and cook over a low heat for a further 5 minutes without browning.

Pour in the wine and chicken stock, bring to a simmer and cook for about 30 minutes or until the artichokes are tender and offer little resistance when a pointed knife is inserted in the base.

Leave the artichokes to cool in the liquor until they are cool enough to handle. Lift them from the liquor – which should be retained – and use a teaspoon to scrape out the choke (5).

Place the de-choked artichokes and their cooking liquor in an airtight container. They can be stored like this in the fridge for up to 4 days if necessary.

FOR THE SAUCE D'ÉPICE Place the oil in a saucepan over a medium heat. When it is hot, add the carrot, onion and all the spices. Cook until the mixture starts to caramelize.

Pour in the white wine to deglaze the pan. Bring to the boil and reduce until the wine has almost evaporated. Add the chicken stock, bring to the boil and simmer until reduced by half.

Allow the sauce to cool slightly, then transfer it to a food processor and liquidize. Pass through a fine sieve into a clean saucepan and add the cream. Bring the sauce to the boil and reduce slightly until the sauce is thick enough to coat the back of the spoon (6).

TO COMPLETE Put 50g/2oz/½ stick of butter in a pan, add the parsnips and cook until golden and soft. Meanwhile, reheat the artichokes in their cooking liquor and adjust the seasoning to taste.

Heat through the confit onions. In another saucepan, wilt the escarole with a little butter and season to taste. Remove the pans of vegetables from the heat. Gently warm the sauce and slice the truffle and foie gras if using.

Place two frying pans over a high heat. As the scallops and foie gras will cook very quickly, you can start to plate up the dishes beforehand. Have ready some warm serving dishes and lay a cooked artichoke in the centre of each. Layer the other vegetables on top and top with the sliced truffle.

When the frying pans are very hot, add some oil to one of them. Season the scallops with salt and pepper and place in the pan. Allow the scallops to brown, which will take 30 seconds, then turn over. Add the butter and remove from the stove so the scallops cook through in the residual heat.

Add the sliced foie gras to the other hot frying pan. This will brown very quickly so you must work fast. When the first side is brown, flip the foie gras over (7), wait for 10 seconds, then take it out of the frying pan.

Remove the scallops from the frying pan and place them on top of the vegetables. Lay the foie gras on top (8).

To finish the sauce, whisk in a little butter to give it texture and shine, then spoon the sauce around the plate and serve immediately.

Chef's notes You can tell scallops
have been soaked when they appear very
white and soft to the touch. It is possible
to buy good shelled scallops that have not
been soaked: ask for what fishmongers call
'dry cut scallop meat'.

Tournedos of Salmon, Spiced Lentils and Foie Gras

Salmon is a versatile fish that can stand up to strong flavours. This dish pairs it with gently spiced lentils and roast foie gras. The flavours are individually simple but immense when mixed together. I prefer to use wild salmon for this dish. Alternatively, I choose organic salmon from Glenarme or Westray, where the fish are free to swim, which keeps the fat content of the flesh low. At a pinch, higher-fat farmed salmon will also work in this recipe. **SERVES 6**

FIG AND APPLE CHUTNEY
1 cooking apple, peeled and cut into 2.5cm/1in dice
20g/¾oz/¼ cup onion, diced
50g/2oz/½ cup dried fig, chopped
25ml/1floz/1½ tbsp white wine vinegar
⅓ tbsp English mustard
a pinch of cayenne pepper
½ clove garlic
50g/2oz/½ cup sultanas
2 tsp sugar

SPICED LENTILS
100g/3½oz/½ cup Umbri or Puy lentils
a pinch of ground cumin
40g/1½oz red onion, finely chopped
25ml/1floz/1½ tbsp balsamic vinegar
1 clove garlic, crushed
20g/¾oz pickled ginger, finely chopped
25ml/1floz/1½ tbsp soy sauce
1 tbsp tomato ketchup
2 tbsp sweet chilli sauce
2 tbsp olive oil
1 tsp chopped coriander (cilantro)
a squeeze of lemon juice

SALMON AND FOIE GRAS
50ml/2floz/¼ cup corn oil
1 salmon fillet, about 1.35kg/3lb
200g/7oz foie gras, cut into 4 slices

HERB CRÈME FRAICHE
100ml/4floz/½ cup crème fraîche
1 tsp chlorophyll (see page 161), or 1 tbsp finely chopped chives and parsley
a squeeze of lime juice
salt and pepper

Thinking ahead The lentils must be soaked overnight before cooking and will take on more of the spice flavour if left overnight once made. The cooked lentil mixture can be stored for up to 4 days in the fridge. The salmon should be prepared a day in advance for the flesh to firm up into cylindrical form. The chutney can be made well in advance and stored in the fridge.

FOR THE CHUTNEY Combine all the ingredients for the chutney in a heavy saucepan. Bring to the boil then lower the heat and simmer for 2 hours until thick. Add a splash of water if the mixture dries out before the 2 hours are up. Leave to cool, then liquidize the mixture until it is the consistency of jam (1). Add the sugar and store chilled.

FOR THE LENTILS Soak the lentils overnight in a bowl of water. Next day, cook the lentils in a pan of fresh boiling salted water for 30 minutes or until tender (if you have hard water on tap, use bottled still water for a better result, see page 165). Drain and leave to cool.

Warm the cumin in a dry saucepan to release the flavour. When fragrant, add the onions, vinegar and garlic. Cook over a medium heat for 10 minutes.

Add the rest of the ingredients, plus the cooked lentils, and stir well. Adjust the seasoning to taste with the lemon juice – you should be able to taste the

acid of the lemon. Remove from the heat, cool completely and store in an airtight container in the fridge until ready to complete the dish.

FOR THE SALMON Check that the salmon is free from pin bones and skin. Trim off the fatty grey flesh on the underside of the fillet.

On a cutting board, lay the fish with the thickest end of the fillet pointing away from you and the tail towards you. Cut a straight line down through the middle of the fish towards the tail at an angle of approximately 30 degrees, giving 2 thin fillets (2).

Place the strips of fish together head to tail on a piece of plastic wrap and wrap into a long tube, expelling all the air (3). Leave to rest for at least 12 hours. To cut the salmon roll into serving portions, take a sharp knife and cut it into cylinders 4cm/1½in wide (4).

FOR THE HERB CRÈME FRIACHE In a small bowl, combine all the ingredients, seasoning to taste with lime juice, salt and pepper.

TO COMPLETE Bring the chuntey to room temperature. In a small saucepan, gently reheat the lentils.

Heat the corn oil in a nonstick frying pan. Season the salmon with salt and pepper. When the oil is hot, place the salmon in the pan and cook until golden brown on each side.

Reduce the heat and cook slowly for 3–4 minutes until there is a thin opaque line running through the center of the fish (5). Remove from the pan and leave to rest for 2 minutes in a warm place.

In the meantime, place a tablespoon of the warmed lentils in the centre of each serving plate. Cut away the plastic wrap from the salmon (6) and place the fish on top of the lentils. Surround the dish with the herb crème fraîche.

Heat a frying pan until very hot. Season the foie gras with salt and pepper, place it in the pan and cook until golden brown on both sides, about 20–30 seconds on each side (7).

Place the foie gras on top of the salmon and finish the dish with a quenelle of chutney before serving.

Chef's notes As an alternative to shaping the salmon into cylinders, you could simply skin and remove the grey flesh from the fillet, then cut it into a square portions of about 90g/3½oz. Cook in the same manner as the cylinders.

John Dory, Braised Lambs' Tongues and Red Wine Emulsion

This dish combines two diverse flavours: slightly sweet and rich lambs' tongues with the subtly earthy sea taste of John Dory. The pairing is enhanced by peppery watercress and sweet onions, so there are many different flavours on the plate, all working together to deliver an exciting taste experience. If you are not keen on lambs' tongues, or are unable to source them, a suitable alternative would be braised rib meat or oxtail. SERVES 4

BRAISED LAMBS' TONGUES

250g/9oz lambs' tongues
60g/2oz/¼ cup sea salt
50ml/2floz/¼ cup corn oil
250g/9oz mirepoix (see page 159)
1 clove garlic
50g/2oz smoked bacon
150ml/5floz/⅔ cup red wine
125ml/4½floz/½ cup lamb jus (see page 156)
250ml/9floz/1 cup chicken stock (see page 157)

2 star anise
150ml/5floz/⅔ cup rice wine vinegar
1 tsp grated stem ginger

RED WINE EMULSION

50ml/2floz/¼ cup corn oil
1.5kg/3lb6oz mirepiox (see page 159)
½ apple, chopped
1 clove garlic, halved
400ml/14floz/1¾ cups red wine

100ml/3½floz/scant ½ cup port
150ml/5floz/⅔ cup chicken stock (see page 157)
200ml/7floz/scant 1 cup semi-skimmed milk
50ml/2floz/¼ cup cream
50g/2oz/½ stick butter
salt and pepper

JOHN DORY

1kg/2lb 4oz John Dory or flounder, cut into 2 fillets
corn oil, for frying

WATERCRESS GARNISH

1 bunch watercress
250g/9oz picked and washed spinach
8 braised shallots (see page 160)
100g/3½oz wild mushrooms
50g/2oz/½ stick butter

Thinking ahead The lambs' tongues must be soaked for 2 days with regular changes of water, and can then be cooked and prepared up to 2 days before serving. The braised shallots can be made up to 3 days before serving and kept in the fridge. The red wine emulsion can be made 1 day in advance and stored chilled.

FOR THE BRAISED TONGUES

Rinse the lambs' tongues and place in 1 litre/1¾ pints/1 quart of cold water with half the salt. Ensure the tongues are immersed and leave overnight. Repeat this process the following day and leave to soak for a second night.

To braise the tongues, heat the oil in a heavy saucepan and fry the mirepoix, garlic and bacon until browned.

Remove the tongues from the soaking water and pat dry. Add to the pan and brown on all sides for about 15 minutes. Add the rest of the ingredients and bring to the boil. Cover with foil and simmer for 3-4 hours over a very low heat until the skin on the tongue peels away easily (1).

Remove the pan from the heat and leave the tongues to cool in the cooking liquor. When cool, peel and trim off any skin and sinew from the tongues leaving a clean piece of meat (2).

Strain the cooking liquor into a clean pan, bring to a boil and boil until the volume of liquid has reduced by half. Add the tongues. then remove from the heat and leave to cool. Place in a covered container in the fridge. They can be stored like this for up to 1 week.

FOR THE RED WINE EMULSION

Heat the oil in a heavy pan. and brown the mirepoix, apple and garlic. Add the wine and port and simmer over a medium heat for 45 minutes.

Strain the wine mixture, then place it in a saucepan with the chicken stock. Bring to the boil and simmer over a moderate heat for 1 hour, or until the volume of liquid has reduced to 200ml/7floz/scant 1 cup and the sauce is a syrupy consistency (3).

Pass the sauce through a strainer and set aside until ready to complete the dish. Alternatively, cool and store in a covered container in the fridge.

TO COMPLETE Ensure the fish fillets are free from scales, then cut each into 2 pieces giving 4 first course portions . Alternatively, leave whole to give 2 main course portions. Pat the fish dry and place in the fridge until needed.

Remove the lamb tongues from the cooking liquor and slice each into 3 pieces. Place the cooking liquor in a small saucepan, add the sliced tongues and braised shallots and place over a low heat to warm through.

Put the red wine emulsion on the stove and heat until the sauce is hot but not steaming – 85°C/185°F is the ideal temperature; do not let it boil. Whisk in the butter, cream and milk.

Place a little butter in a frying pan, add the wild mushrooms and cook for 1-2 minutes or until soft.

Add the spinach and watercress. When they have wilted, transfer the contents of the pan to the tongue mixture and adjust the seasoning to taste. Cover the pan with plastic wrap or a lid and set aside in a warm place.

Heat a little oil in a nonstick frying pan. Season the fish and, when the oil is hot, place it in the pan skin-side down and cook until golden brown, which will take about 1 minute. Turn the fillets, add a little butter to the pan and cook on the other side – dory cooks quickly so take care not to cook it for longer than 3 minutes in total.

Place the meat mixture in the centre of some serving plates. Drain the fish and lay it on top. Using a whisk or electric hand blender, whisk the red wine emulsion until a cappuccino-like foam appears (4), then spoon the froth over the plates and serve immediately.

Chef's notes
These quantities could also be served as a main course for two. The lamb tongues can be replaced by braised rib meat (see page 88). The wine for this recipe should be a full-bodied red, not necessarily expensive. The dish can be finished with a drizzle of lemon oil if you wish to give it an extra zing (page 162).

Roast Squab, Fresh Peas and Garlic Cream

I like the subtle gamey flavour of squab. It is rich but versatile and generally more interesting than chicken. Squab is

available year-round thanks to successful farming practices; it is also simple and quick to cook. Although this dish is

elaborately flavoured, a good result is easily achieved because very little is done to alter the natural taste of the

ingredients. When combined, they are clean, pure and well balanced — a splendid first course. SERVES 4

FRESH PEA AND TRUFFLE EMULSION

4 tsp water
4 tsp double (heavy) cream
125g/4½oz/½ cup butter
½ tsp truffle oil
1 small truffle, finely sliced
   into 8–12 pieces
200g/7oz/1½ cups fresh peas
1 tsp chopped tarragon
2 rashers unsmoked back
   bacon, chopped

GARLIC CREAM

3 cloves garlic
sea salt
a splash of olive oil
25ml/1floz/1½ tbsp double
   (heavy) cream
200ml/7floz/scant 1 cup
   skimmed milk
25g/1oz/¼ stick butter

SQUAB AND FOIE GRAS

2 squab, legs removed
200g/7oz foie gras
25ml/1floz/1½ tbsp corn oil
25g/1oz/¼ stick butter
salt and pepper

TO FINISH

12 black trompette
   mushrooms, rehydrated
   if dried
a little strawberry dressing
   (see page 163)

Thinking ahead You will need to pre-order the squab from your butcher, and find a good supplier of fresh foie gras. The garlic can be roasted, pounded to a paste and stored in an airtight container in the fridge for 6-8 hours before finishing the sauce.

FOR THE PEAS Half-fill a pot with water and add a handful of salt. Bring to a rolling boil. Meanwhile, place about 6 ice-cubes in a container and fill with cold water to stop the cooking.

Place the peas in the water and simmer until they are just cooked, firm but with no crunch. Immediately remove the peas from the heat and plunge them into the ice-bath (1).

When cold, drain the peas thoroughly and place them in a covered container in the fridge until ready to complete.

FOR THE GARLIC CREAM Heat the oven to 180°C/350°F/Gas 4. Place the garlic cloves on a sheet of foil about 15cm/6in square. Sprinkle with some sea salt and drizzle with the olive oil. Seal the edges of the foil to form an airtight package. Place in the oven for 25-30 minutes, or until the garlic cloves are soft when squeezed (2). Cook them further if necessary.

Remove the garlic from the oven and allow cool slightly. Peel the cloves, then place them in a mortar and pound to a paste with the pestle (3).

In a small saucepan, bring the milk, cream and butter to a boil. Add the garlic and blitz with a hand blender until smooth. Adjust the seasoning to taste, then cover with plastic wrap and keep warm until ready to serve.

FOR THE TRUFFLE EMULSION Place the water in a small saucepan and bring to the boil, then add the cream and bring back to the boil.

Turn the heat right down under the pan. Dice the butter into 1cm/½in cubes and, when the liquid has come off the boil, slowly whisk the butter piece by piece into the cream mixture, ensuring an emulsion is achieved after each addition of butter (4). Under no circumstances should the sauce be allowed to boil.

TO COMPLETE Heat the oven to 180°C/350°F/Gas 4. Place a frying pan on the stove and heat the oil. Cook the squabs on all sides until golden (5).

Transfer to a roasting tin placing the birds breast down. Roast for 4 minutes, then turn the squabs over and cook for more 4 minutes, adding the trompettes to the roasting tin after the birds have been roasting for 7 minutes in total.

Meanwhile, heat the truffle emulsion with the peas, bacon, tarragon, truffle and 4-5 drops of truffle oil, being careful not to let the sauce boil.

5

6

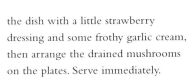

7

8

Take a clean frying pan and heat it to a high temperature. While it is heating, take the squabs from the oven and set aside to rest for 4 minutes.

Place the trompettes on paper towel to drain. Using a whisk or electric hand blender, froth the garlic cream until cappuccino-like, then allow it to settle.

Remove the squab breasts from the bone (6) and slice each breast into 3 pieces (7). Take 4 warm serving plates and place a pile of pea mixture on each, adding some more truffle oil. Place the squab on the pea mixture.

In the hot frying pan, sear the foie gras until golden brown on each side (8). Lay it on top of the squab. Garnish the dish with a little strawberry dressing and some frothy garlic cream, then arrange the drained mushrooms on the plates. Serve immediately.

Chef's notes It is important not to overcook the squab, which needs only 8 minutes cooking and 4 minutes resting. If you do not have fresh truffles, use a good truffle oil instead. Frozen peas can be used in place of fresh if the latter are unavailable.

Terrine of Free Range Chicken and Foie Gras

A terrine reveals the true quality of the restaurant kitchen. Some say a good kitchen can be marked on its terrine, as there are so many different cooking techniques involved. This recipe is the result of 3 years development and evolution to get the taste and presentation right, and I'm sure it will take another 3 years before I am truly happy with it. I have suggested serving this version with sweet dried figs and parsnip purée, both of which offset the slightly bitter undertones contributed by the foie gras and mushrooms. **MAKES 10 PORTIONS**

TERRINE
700g/1lb8oz lobe foie gras
100g/3½oz dried haricot
   blanc, or similar beans,
   soaked overnight
300ml/11floz/1⅓ cups
   corn oil
3 x 1.2kg/1lb11oz free
   range chickens, legs
   removed
2 savoy cabbages

300ml/11floz/1⅓ cups lamb
   jus (see page 156)
20 medium shiitake
   mushrooms
3 cloves garlic
4 sprigs thyme
200ml/7floz/¾ cup red wine
100g/3½oz black trompette,
   or other wild mushrooms
4 globe artichokes, cooked
   as per recipe on page 36,
   omitting the carrots and
   onions

200g/7oz semi-dried grapes
200ml/7floz/¾ cup duck
   or goose fat
12 thin slices Parma ham

PARSNIP PURÉE
1kg/2lb4oz parsnips
275ml/10floz/1¼ cups milk
275ml/10floz/1¼ cups
   water
50g/2oz/½ stick butter
salt and pepper

DRIED FIGS
3 ripe figs
icing (confectioners') sugar,
   for dusting

TO FINISH
sprigs of chervil
4 tsp truffle dressing (see
   page 163)

Thinking ahead You need to start this dish well in advance of serving and it tastes best when left in the fridge to mature for 2-3 days. Source a good supplier for the free-range chickens and foie gras. The grapes need to be dried for 7-10 days (depending on humidity), but this simply involves laying them on a tray lined with parchment paper and leaving in a dry place. The artichokes can be cooked 3-4 days in advance. The lamb jus can be made well ahead and stored in the freezer. Soak the beans overnight before cooking.

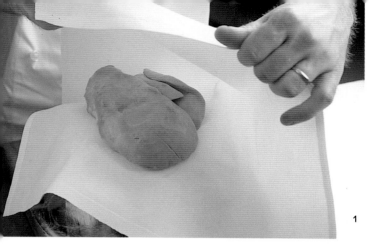

1

2

3

4

FOR THE TERRINE Place the foie gras on an upturned bowl covered with a damp dish towel (1) and leave it at room temperature for 2 hours to bring the foie gras to a workable temperature. The liver should open under its own weight to give 2 sides to the lobe and reveal some blood vessels, fat and sinew.

Meanwhile, cook the soaked beans in a pan of salted, soft tap water or bottled still water for 45-50 minutes at a very gentle simmer. When the beans are tender, drain and refresh them gently in cold water. Store in a covered container until ready to use.

Heat the oven to 180°C/350°F/Gas 4. Place a frying pan on the stove and add

about 50ml/2floz/¼ cup of corn oil. Take the 3 chickens, season well and fry them 1 or 2 at a time in the pan until sealed and golden all over (2).

Transfer the chickens to a baking tray and roast them for 18-20 minutes until cooked through. Remove from the oven and leave to cool breast-side down to ensure the juices run into the breast and not out through the carcass. Turn the oven down to 60°C/140°F/Gas ¼.

Place a large pan of water on the stove with a handful of salt and bring to the

boil. Half-fill a large bowl with water and add a handful of ice cubes.

Discard any damaged or very thick leaves from the cabbage, then remove about 2 layers of the remaining outer leaves. Trim off the central branch of each leaf, leaving two tender sides.

Wash the leaves, then cook them for 2 minutes in the boiling salted water until tender but still green. Plunge into the ice bath to stop the cooking, then drain. Trim or 'square-off' the leaves to give a rectangle (3) and set aside.

In a small saucepan, warm the lamb jus. Meanwhile, place a large frying pan over a high heat. Add 150ml/5floz/½ cup of corn oil and lay in the shiitake tops down, plus the garlic and thyme (4).

Cook the shiitake for 1–2 minutes, then add the red wine, warm lamb jus, and the rest of the prepared mushrooms. Bring to a boil, then remove the pan from the heat and let the mushrooms to cool in the sauce.

Lay a sheet of plastic wrap on a work surface and place the soft, open foie

gras onto it carefully. With a small sharp knife, remove the main artery that divides the two halves of the lobe (5). Carefully ease out the rest of the veins that run through the liver. Cut the foie gras carefully in to 5cm/2in strips, wrap in plastic and set aside in a cool place.

TO BUILD THE TERRINE Cover a work surface with a double layer of plastic wrap measuring 30 x 45cm/ 12 x 18in. Use this to line the terrine mould, expelling any air (6).

Make sure all the terrine ingredients are just above room temperature and have a large metal tray next to you while building the terrine to hold each ingredient at each stage.

Remove the chicken breasts from the bone (7) and trim off any fat, sinew and skin. Cut the breasts into 3 lengthways (8) and place in the tray.

Strain the mushrooms, retaining the liquor. Discard the garlic and thyme. Place the mushrooms on the tray.

If the artichokes are cold, warm them in a little of their cooking liquor in a microwave oven for 30 seconds. Cut them in half and place on the tray.

Place the beans and cabbage leaves on the tray with the semi-dried grapes

In a small pan, heat the duck or goose fat until it just melts. Pour this over all the ingredients in the tray (9) and season well.

Lay the foie gras on a baking tray lined with paper towel, ensuring some space is left between each piece. Place in the low oven for 6 minutes, then remove and set aside.

The way in which the terrine is built is up to you, but there are 2 rules that must be followed. Firstly, strips of cabbage the exact width of the terrine must be placed on the bottom and at the top. Secondly, you need to brush each layer with the lamb jus. Otherwise, simply layer all the ingredients except the ham in the terrine (10) until they rise above the mould by 2.5cm/1in.

When the terrine is full and topped with the cabbage (11), fold over the plastic wrap lining the terrine and seal tightly. Wrap the whole terrine with another piece of plastic.

Using a sharp knife, pierce small holes in the plastic along the edge of the terrine 1cm/½in apart to allow the excess juices to escape while the terrine is pressing (12).

Place a weight, such as some bottles of milk sitting in a baking pan, on top of the terrine to press it down (13). The weight should be about as heavy as a common house brick and must fit right across the top of the mould.

Place the weighted terrine in the fridge with a tray underneath to catch the juices that will ooze out during pressing. Ensure the weight is level and secure, then leave overnight.

Next day, remove the terrine from the fridge and carefully unwrap it. Trim off any overhang at the top of the terrine to make the sides square.

On a work surface, lay 6 pieces of Parma ham on a sheet of plastic wrap and sit the terrine on this (14). Lay the other 6 slices of ham on top of the terrine (15), then press the ham against the terrine and wrap tightly with the plastic. Chill for 2–3 days before serving.

FOR THE DRIED FIGS With the stems pointing upwards, square off the sides of the figs and cut each one into 2 thick slices. Place the slices on a sheet of parchment paper and dust them with a little icing sugar.

Leave the fig slices to dry overnight in a dry place, until the texture is that of candied fruit (16). Store them in an airtight container until required.

FOR THE PARSNIP PURÉE Peel and chop the parsnips. Place them in a large saucepan with the milk and water. Bring to the boil and cook until the parsnips are soft. Drain thoroughly.

Transfer the cooked parsnips to a food processor and blend until smooth. Place the purée in a clean saucepan with the butter, return to the heat and cook, stirring, until thick.

14

13

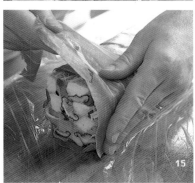

15

16

Taste the parsnip purée and adjust the seasoning. Remember that it will be served cold, so should be slightly over-seasoned to compensate for the cooler temperature. Store the parsnip purée in an airtight container until ready for use – it can be stored for up to 4 days in the fridge if necessary.

TO COMPLETE Leaving the plastic on the terrine, slice it into portions 1cm/½in thick. Lay on the serving plates, then remove the plastic.

Using 2 spoons, shape a quenelle of parsnip purée (17-18) for each serving and place on the plates. Top the purée with some dried fig. Garnish with the dressing and chervil and serve.

Chef's notes This dish is the hardest and most complex dish in the book. The secret of success is time and patience. The temperatures, cooking times and wrapping all need to be accurate to achieve a perfect result. If you are attempting to make this terrine at home, my advice is to read this recipe over a few times to be familiar with each step before starting. Make sure that you have assembled all the necessary equipment, and that you have enough time to work carefully on each stage.

17

18

Main Courses

Salmon Mi Cuit, Horseradish Sauce

The term 'mi cuit' is directly translated as 'just cooked' and that is what this salmon is. The cooking oil must not rise far above the temperature at which the protein in the fish sets if the flesh is to remain soft. With a higher heat the proteins will harden and make the fish tough. Pairing horseradish and tangy pickled beetroot with salmon makes a sharp contrast to the fattiness naturally found in the fish. SERVES 4

COOKING OIL
500ml/18floz/2¼ cups
   olive oil
750ml/1 pint 6floz/3½ cups
   corn oil
2 star anise
2 bay leaves
3 used vanilla beans
20 peppercorns

SALMON
4 pieces salmon fillet, about
   120g/4½oz each, trimmed
   of skin and grey fat

BEETROOT PURÉE
1 x 340g/12oz jar pickled
   beetroot
2 tsp red wine vinegar

CABBAGE
50ml/2floz/¼ cup olive oil
50g/2oz/½ stick butter
2 large or 4 small shallots,
   finely diced
2 cloves garlic, chopped and
   sprout removed
1 large carrot, peeled and
   thinly sliced
2 sprigs thyme

1 bay leaf
50ml/2floz/¼ cup water
50ml/2floz/¼ cup fish stock
   (see page 157)
1 savoy cabbage, finely sliced
   and stalks removed

HORSERADISH SAUCE
200g/7oz/1 cup dry mashed
   potato, made from about
   225g/8oz potatoes, peeled
1 tbsp creamed horseradish
a little cream
a little butter
salt and pepper

BEETROOT FOAM
100ml/4floz/½ cup fish
   stock (see page 157)
1 x 340g/12oz jar pickled
   beetroot
100ml/4floz/½ cup
   skimmed milk
4 tsp double (heavy) cream
50g/2oz/½ stick butter

Thinking ahead Organic or wild salmon is preferable. Order from your fishmonger in good time. If using home-made fish stock, make it the day before. You also need pre-mashed potatoes for this recipe, which can be prepared 1 day ahead. The cooking oil needs to infuse for at least 24 hours. The cabbage can be made the day before but is ideally cooked on the day of serving.

FOR THE COOKING OIL Place all the ingredients in a saucepan (1) and heat slowly to about 60°C/140°F. Leave on the heat to infuse for 1 hour. Remove from the pan and keep at room temperature for at least 24 hours.

FOR THE BEETROOT PURÉE Place the beetroot and pickling juice in a food processor and blend to a purée. Remove and wrap in a piece of muslin or cheesecloth and allow the excess juice to drip out (2). When the mixture is very thick, place it in a bowl and stir in the red wine vinegar. Store chilled.

FOR THE CABBAGE Place a large pan with a tight-fitting lid over a medium heat. Add the oil and butter and heat gently, then add the shallots, garlic and carrot and cook for 2 minutes without letting them brown. Add the thyme, bay leaf and cabbage to the pan and cook for 3 minutes, again without browning.

Pour in the water and fish stock. Cover and steam for 3 minutes. If serving immediately, drain, then adjust the seasoning to taste and serve. Otherwise spread the cabbage out thinly on a tray to cool, then store covered in the fridge for up to 24 hours.

FOR THE HORSERADISH SAUCE Combine the mashed potato and horseradish in a saucepan over a low heat. Add the cream and butter slowly until you have a mixture the consistency of a thick, puréed soup. Adjust the seasoning to taste and keep warm

FOR THE BEETROOT FOAM In a small saucepan, bring the fish stock to a boil and boil hard until it has reduced to a glacé (3). Add the pickled beetroot, and the juice from the jar, and heat slightly. Add the milk, cream and butter.

Transfer to a food processor and purée until smooth. It may foam up, but do not worry as this is normal. Return to the saucepan and keep warm without letting the sauce boil.

TO COMPLETE In a large saucepan, or skillet heat the infused cooking oil to 35-40°C/95-104°F using a digital probe thermometer to maintain the temperature and moving the pan on and off the stove to ensure it does not get too hot. Alternatively, set the oven to the lowest possible temperature and place the oil in an ovenproof dish in the oven to achieve a similar result.

When the oil is at the required temperature, lay the salmon pieces in it and cook for 40 minutes. When done, the flesh will still be pink-orange (4) but do not let this worry you as it is cooked perfectly. Remove from the oil and set aside to drain.

In the meantime, reheat the cabbage as necessary in a small saucepan and warm through the horseradish sauce.

Place the cabbage on serving plates, the salmon on top, then season with sea salt. Top with the beetroot purée (5). Spoon the potato and horseradish sauce around the plate. Using a whisk or electric hand blender, whip up the warm beetroot foam (6), spoon the bubbles around the plate and serve.

Chef's notes The method I have
used to cook the fish here can be adopted
for most fish, including turbot, sole, bass
and halibut. You can also experiment with
other spices to infuse in the oil.

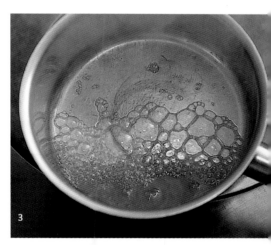

3

2

4

5

Sea Bass, Crab Beignet and Fennel

This dish is clean, fresh and exciting to eat. All the different flavours and textures – crisp skin, delicate bass and beignet of crab – work well together. Seabass and fennel are often considered a good match. Here the fennel is made into a cream so that the taste is softened and does not overwhelm any of the other ingredients. SERVES 4

CRAB BEIGNET
100g/4oz fish mousse (see page 159)
100g/4oz cooked white crabmeat, pinked over
4 flowering courgettes (zucchini)
1 batch tempura batter (see page 163)
corn oil, for deep-frying
plain flour, for dusting

TOMATO FONDU
6 ripe plum tomatoes
1 large shallot, finely chopped
75ml/3floz/⅓ cup olive oil
½ clove garlic, crushed
½ tsp chopped coriander (cilantro)

CAPER DRESSING
1 tbsp fine capers
5 tbsp aged balsamic vinegar
5 tbsp lemon oil (see page 162)

FENNEL CREAM
1 bulb fennel
1 clove garlic, crushed
50ml/2floz/¼ cup corn oil
100ml/4floz/½ cup fish or chicken stock (see page 157)
100ml/4floz/½ cup cream
50g/2oz/½ stick butter

VEGETABLES
8 asparagus spears
100g/4oz extra fine green beans
8 medium fresh shiitake mushrooms, halved

SEA BASS
4 pieces wild sea bass fillet, about 130g/4½oz each, trimmed of scales and bones
50ml/2floz/¼ cup corn oil
50g/2oz/½ stick butter
salt and pepper

TO FINISH
50ml/2floz/¼ cup corn oil
50g/2oz/½ stick butter

Thinking ahead The tomato fondu, fennel cream, caper dressing and tempura batter can be made only 2 hours in advance of serving and kept at room temperature. The fish mousse used to fill the beignets can be made the day before serving.

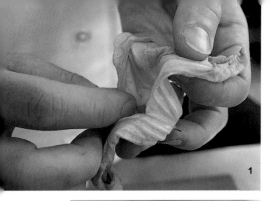

1

2

3

FOR THE CRAB BEIGNET

Gently break off the flowers from the courgettes, ensuring they stay intact. Carefully snap out and discard the stigma from the flowers (1). Reserve the courgettes and flowers separately.

Place the fish mousse in a bowl and mix in the crab. Season lightly.

Take a small amount of the mousse and place it in some plastic wrap, wrapping it tightly into a ball. Bring a small pan of water to a simmer, add the ball of mousse and test-poach (2). Taste and adjust the seasoning as necessary.

When you are satisfied with the mousse, place it in a disposable piping bag. Gently open the flowers a little and pipe in the mousse, filling the flower half full. Alternatively, use a

teaspoon to half-fill the flowers with mousse. Twist the ends of the petals to seal in the mousse (3).

Place the filled flowers in a steaming basket over a pan of boiling water. Steam for 2–3 minutes until firm, then carefully immerse them in a bowl of iced water to stop the cooking.

Remove the beignets from the water, pat dry and store in an airtight container the fridge for up to 2 hours.

FOR THE TOMATO FONDU Bring

a large saucepan of water to the boil and prepare an ice-bath. Core the tomatoes and mark a cross in the rounded end of each one. Place them in the boiling water for 8–10 seconds, then remove immediately and place in the ice bath to arrest the cooking.

When the tomatoes are cold, peel and cut into quarters. Remove the seeds and place on kitchen paper to dry (4).

Heat the olive oil in a saucepan, add the shallot and crushed garlic and cook for 2–3 minutes without browning.

Meanwhile, cut the tomato flesh into 1cm/½in dice and add to the shallots. Cook for a further 1–2 minutes until the tomato starts to soften. Adjust the seasoning to taste, add the coriander, then remove from the pan and set aside in a covered container.

FOR THE CAPER DRESSING In

a small bowl, combine all the dressing ingredients. Whisk together, adjust the seasoning to taste and set aside.

FOR THE FENNEL CREAM

Trim the fennel bulb, removing any blemishes, and finely chop it.

Heat the oil in a saucepan, add the chopped fennel and crushed garlic and cook slowly over a moderate heat for 6–7 minutes without browning.

Add the fish stock, raise the heat under the pan and boil until the volume of liquid has reduced by half. Pour in the cream, return to the boil and simmer until reduced by half again. Remove the pan from the heat and allow the mixture to cool slightly.

Transfer to a food processor and purée until fine. Return the sauce to a clean pan and set aside in a warm place. The butter should be whisked into the sauce only just before serving.

FOR THE VEGETABLES Slice the reserved courgettes. Bring a large pan of water to the boil and prepare an ice-bath. Blanch the courgettes for 1–2 minutes, then refresh in the iced water. Repeat with the asparagus and

green beans, cooking them separately. Drain the vegetables well and place in a covered container in the fridge.

TO COMPLETE Heat the oil for deep-frying to 180°C/350°F and have the crab beignets, a dish of plain flour and the tempura batter ready next to it.

Meanwhile, heat 50ml/2floz/¼ cup of corn oil in a frying pan over a medium heat. Add the shiitake and cook for 1 minute, then add the butter and let it melt. Add the blanched green vegetables and cook for 1 minute. Adjust the seasoning to taste and remove the pan from the heat. Keep warm while the fish is cooking.

Ensure the sea bass is free of bones and scales. Take a nonstick frying pan large enough to comfortably hold all 4 of the fish fillets and place it over a medium-high heat .

Add 50ml/2floz/¼ cup corn oil. Season the bass on the flesh side and carefully place it in the pan skin-side down. Cook for 2 minutes, then turn over and cook for another 1–2 minutes.

Add the butter, reduce the heat to very low and allow to rest until the fish is just cooked and firm to the touch.

Place a mound of the tomato fondu on one side of each plate and then arrange the vegetable mixture in the centre.

Roll the crab beignets in the plain flour, shake off the excess (5), then dip them into the batter. Place all the beignets in the fryer and cook for 1 minute until golden brown (6).

Meanwhile, drain the fish and place it on top of the vegetables. Remove the beignets from the oil, drain briefly on some paper towel and place them on top of the tomato fondu.

Whisk the butter into the warm fennel cream, then garnish the plates with the fennel cream and caper dressing and serve immediately.

Chef's notes You may prefer to cook the vegetables around 20 minutes before serving, then reheat them in a microwave when needed, allowing you to concentrate fully on the fish and beignet, which are both easy to overcook.

Turbot, Braised Ox Tail, Parsley and Lemon Oil

This dish has been with me for a number of years in many forms, although the combination of turbot and ox tail has remained the same. It works because the fish and ox tail are both meaty, and white fish – like red meat – is classically served with a red wine sauce. The combination produces a very robust taste, while the lemon and parsley oils and sherry vinegar help cut through the richness. SERVES 4

BRAISED OX TAIL
plain flour, for dusting
1kg/2lb4oz ox tail, cut into small rounds
70ml/3floz/⅓ cup corn oil
1 small onion, chopped
1 carrot, chopped
1 stick celery, chopped
1 leek, roughly chopped
1 tbsp tomato paste
2 cloves garlic, halved
2 sprigs thyme
1 bay leaf
750ml/25floz bottle full-bodied red wine
500ml/18floz/2¼ cups chicken stock (see page 157)
500ml/18floz/2¼ cups lamb jus (see page 156)
4 tsp sherry vinegar

LITTLE GEMS
2 heads little gem lettuce, halved lengthways
25ml/1floz/1½ tbsp corn oil
50ml/2floz/¼ cup orange juice
25g/1oz/¼ stick butter
50ml/2floz/¼ cup fish stock (see page 157)

HERB MASH
200g/7oz/1 cup mashed potato, made from about 225g/8oz potatoes, peeled
1 tsp chlorophyll (see page 161) or finely chopped herbs
a little butter
a little cream

TURBOT
4 pieces turbot fillet, about 120g/4½oz each
25g/1oz/¼ stick butter
25ml/1floz/1½ tbsp corn oil
salt and pepper

TO FINISH
12 confit onions (see page 160)
120g/4oz mixed wild or cultivated mushrooms
2 tsps herb oil (see page 161)
2 tsps lemon oil (see page 162)
2 tsps truffle dressing (see page 163)
chive tips and chervil sprigs, to garnish

Thinking ahead Pre-order your fish and meat. Have the turbot filleted, skinned and trimmed by the fishmonger and ask the butcher to cut the ox tail into small rounds. The stocks can be made well in advance and frozen. The ox tail can be braised and taken off the bone 3-4 days before serving as long as it is stored in the cooking liquor. The lemon and herb oils can be made 3-4 days in advance, or earlier if stored in the freezer. The truffle dressing and confit onions can be made 2 days ahead. The little gems can be cooked 1 day in advance while the mashed potato can be made 3 hours before serving and should be kept at room temperature.

FOR THE BRAISED OX TAIL Set the oven to 140°C/275°F/Gas 1. In a large frying pan, heat the corn oil over a moderate heat.

Dust the ox tail in a little plain flour (1) and place in the pan 2 or 3 pieces at a time to prevent steaming. Fry the ox tail on each side until browned (2), then place in a large casserole.

Add the vegetables and tomato paste to the frying pan, with a little more oil if necessary. Cook for 10-12 minutes, then place them in the casserole with the garlic, thyme and bay.

Deglaze the pan with the red wine (3), stirring vigorously. Bring to a boil and simmer until reduced by half. Add the lamb jus and stock and pour the mixture into the casserole.

Add the rest of the ingredients to the casserole, then pour in as much water as is necessary to ensure that all of the ingredients are covered.

Cover the casserole with a tight-fitting lid or some foil and place in the oven to cook. Check after 2½ hours to ensure there is still enough liquid to cover the ingredients.

When done, after about 3 hours, the meat should just fall off the bone but still retain its moisture (4). Remove the casserole from the oven. Place the ox tails on a plate, cover with plastic wrap to keep them moist, and cool slightly.

Strain the cooking liquor into a large saucepan, and place over a high heat. Bring to a boil and reduce to a syrupy consistency, ensuring that the sauce does not burn on the base of the pan. Skim the surface as necessary.

Pick the meat off the bone, trimming off any fat and sinew and keeping the meat pieces as large as possible (5), about 1cm/½in long. Place the meat in a covered container and set aside.

When the sauce has reduced, pour it over the ox tails. Allow to cool slightly, then store covered in the fridge; it will keep well for 3-4 days like this.

FOR THE LITTLE GEMS Take a frying pan large enough to fit the 4 halves of little gem comfortably. Place the empty pan over a medium heat, add the oil, then the little gems and cook until slightly browned, taking care not to scorch the leaves.

Add the butter to the pan and cook until it foams (6) and turns nut brown. Pour in the orange juice and fish stock to deglaze the pan, then cover loosely with foil and simmer the little gems for 4-5 minutes or until the core of the lettuce starts to soften.

Remove the lettuce from the pan and keep warm until serving, or allow to cool and store in the fridge for up to 1 day. Retain some of the cooking liquor for reheating.

FOR THE HERB MASH Place the mashed potato in a saucepan over a medium heat and add the chlorophyll or chopped herbs. Add a little butter and cream to adjust the consistency as desired, then season to taste and keep the mash warm until serving time.

TO COMPLETE Have the truffle dressing, lemon oil and herb oil ready. If you have stored the braised ox tail, remove it from the fridge, place it in a small saucepan and reheat carefully ensuring that the syrupy liquid does not burn. Just before serving, add a little sherry vinegar – just enough so that you can taste a little acid in the sauce but can't quite tell what it is.

Heat a small frying pan, add 2 tbsp of corn oil, then the mushrooms. Sauté

5

the mushrooms until slightly coloured, then add 50g/2oz/½ stick of butter and cook until foaming. Remove from the heat, drain and keep warm.

Heat the confit onions and keep them warm. Bring the baby gem and herb mash up to serving temperature, which will take 1–2 minutes in a covered pan over a medium heat.

Place a frying pan that will hold all 4 turbot fillets over a medium heat and add 50ml/2floz/¼ cup of corn oil. Season the fish with salt and ground white pepper, place in the pan and

cook until golden brown on one side. Turn, then reduce the heat and cook for a further 2 or so minutes – the exact time will depend on the thickness of fillet. To test for doneness, press the fish; it should have just a little give in the flesh (7). Alternatively, if you prefer fish to be cooked through, keep cooking until the flesh is firm.

Place a spoonful of herb mash in the center of the serving plate and top with half a little gem. Surround with the warm mushrooms and onions.

Spoon over a little of the ox tail and sauce (8), then place the cooked fish on top and drizzle more sauce around plate. Finish by dripping both flavoured oils (9) and the truffle dressing around the fish, then garnish with herbs.

Chef's notes As an alternative to the turbot, john dory or flounder can be used, or even cod. If using cod, salt it the day before serving, as in the recipe for clam chowder (see page 15).

6

7

8

9

Roast Organic Chicken, Wild Mushroom Risotto

The essence of this dish is flavour enhancement and flavour extraction. The instructions have been carefully devised to give the maximum taste sensations. This is achieved with fresh ingredients and particular cooking methods, including the manner in which the chicken is rested and how the leeks are chopped down for the cream. The steps are all simple, but when executed properly, the results are amazing. **SERVES 6**

RISOTTO

1 litre/1¾ pints/4½ cups
   chicken stock (see page
   157), plus 200ml/7floz/
   1 cup chicken stock
50ml/2floz/¼ cup corn oil
2 shallots, finely chopped
½ clove garlic, halved
250g/9oz/1¼ cups carnaroli
   or arborio rice
4 tbsp white wine
250g/9oz mixed wild
   mushrooms
2 tsp chopped chives

50g/2oz/½ cup parmesan
   cheese, grated
75g/3oz/¾ stick butter
salt and pepper
truffle oil, to season
   (optional)

CHICKEN

250g/9oz/2¼ sticks butter,
   softened
3 organic chickens, about
   1.3kg/2lb13oz each, legs
   removed

8 medium sorrel leaves, or
   equivalent, cut into fine
   strips
2 lemons
1 bulb garlic
1 bunch thyme
3 bay leaves
50ml/2floz/¼ cup corn oil

LEEK CREAM

3 leeks, trimmed
200ml/7floz/1 cup double
   (heavy) cream

CHICKEN GRAVY

200ml/7floz/1 cup chicken
   stock (see page 157)
1 sprig thyme

GARNISH

a few sprigs soft herbs
18 spears green asparagus
50ml/2floz/¼ cup truffle
   dressing (see page 163)
12 confit button onions
   (see page 160)
1 savoy cabbage

Thinking ahead The chicken with sorrel butter can be prepared 1 day in advance if necessary. The risotto base can be made only 6-8 hours before serving. You can also relieve last-minute pressure by blanching and refreshing the greens 2-3 hours in advance and keeping them in the fridge. If desired, make the truffle dressing and confit onions 2 days before and store chilled.

FOR THE RISOTTO BASE In a saucepan, bring 1 litre/1¾ pints/4½ cups of chicken stock to a simmer. In a separate, heavy pan, heat the corn oil over a medium heat and sweat the shallots and garlic for 3 minutes without letting them brown. Add the rice and sweat for a further 2 minutes, again without colouring.

Pour in the wine and simmer until it has reduced to a glaze. Begin adding the stock in small increments of about 50-75ml/2-3floz/¼-⅓ cup (1). Bring the risotto back to the boil each time, allowing the stock to evaporate while stirring continuously. Each process of adding and simmering will take about 3 minutes. Repeat several times until the rice is nearly cooked but not chalky to the bite – in total it should take about 14 minutes from the first addition of chicken stock.

Remove the risotto from the pan, ensuring the rice is reasonably dry (2). Spread it over a tray (3) and allow to cool. The risotto can be stored like this in the fridge for 6-8 hours.

FOR THE CHICKEN Place the softened butter in a bowl and mix in the shredded sorrel (4). Take the chicken and slightly ease the skin away from the wishbone area (5). Gently force around one-third of the butter into the first 2.5/1in or so of the breast where the skin has been eased away (6). Smooth over to give a flat surface (7). Repeat this process for the other 2 chickens and the remaining butter.

Cut each lemon in half, divide the garlic bulb into 3 batches and place some lemon and garlic in the cavity of each chicken. Divide the thyme between them. Wrap in plastic wrap

and store in the fridge – it can be left overnight but must be tightly wrapped to ensure the garlic is not invasive.

The chickens will take approximately 25 minutes to cook on an oven temperature of 170°C/325°F/Gas 3, then they will need 5 minutes to rest and 5 minutes to prepare for serving: bear this in mind when judging the completion time of the dish. It will be best to prepare and cook the leek cream while the chickens are roasting.

To cook the chickens, place a roasting tray or large pan over a moderate heat and add the corn oil. When hot, place the chickens in the roasting pan, breast side down at a 45 degree angle. Cook for 2-3 minutes, then tilt the chickens to the other side to ensure an even colour on each of the breasts (8).

When the chicken breasts are light brown but not golden, turn them so

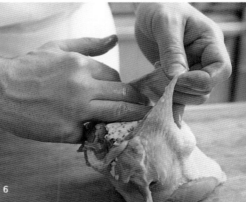

the breasts are facing upwards. Place in the oven and cook for 20-25 minutes, basting every 10 minutes. Check for doneness by pinching the fattest part of the breast with your forefinger and thumb (9). It should feel quite firm. Cook further if required.

When the chickens are completely cooked, remove them from the oven and place breast-side down so the juices seep into the meat and not out onto the tray. Pour half the melted butter in the tray into the cavities to ensure extra basting, then set aside to rest for 5 minutes before removing the meat from the carcasses.

FOR THE LEEK CREAM Finely chop the leeks (10), to maximize the flavour extraction. Place them in a medium saucepan with the butter and

cook over a low heat for 20-30 minutes until they become semi-translucent. Add the cream and cook until firm without letting the mixture colour.

Allow the leek cream to cool slightly, then transfer to a food processor and blend for 1-2 minutes on full power until you have a firm mass (11). Set aside in a warm place until ready to serve. Do not let the mixture cool completely as reheating it could potentially split the reduced cream.

FOR THE CHICKEN GRAVY Take the tray in which the chickens were roasted, pour about half the fat into a small saucepan and set aside. Discard the remaining fat but keep the sediment and juices in the bottom of the tray.

Place over a high heat. Add the thyme and pour the chicken stock into

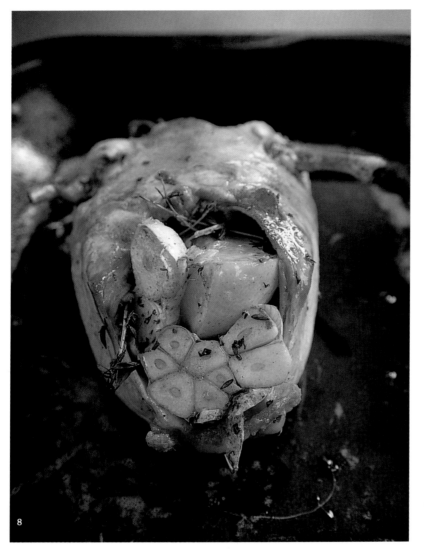

the tray, working off all the sediment from the bottom with a wooden spoon (12). Bring to the boil, then transfer the liquid, sediment included, to a saucepan. Return to the boil and simmer until the volume of liquid has reduced by half.

Pass the gravy through a fine sieve and into a clean saucepan. There will be a certain amount of fat on top of the gravy – don't worry, this is where the most of the flavour is and it really adds to the quality of the finished dish. Cover the pan with plastic wrap and set aside until ready to serve.

FOR THE GARNISH Place a large pot of water on the stove with a scant handful of salt and bring to the boil. Meanwhile, prepare an ice bath for refreshing the green vegetables.

Cut the root off the cabbage, break off the leaves and wash. Slice the leaves into 1cm/½in strips then blanch for 1 minute in the boiling water. Remove with a perforated spoon (13).

Refresh in the ice bath, then remove and drain. Repeat this process with the asparagus, blanching it for 1½ minutes before plunging into the ice bath. Set both vegetables aside until assembly.

TO COMPLETE In the pan the chicken fat was reserved in, place the blanched asparagus, cabbage and confit onions and warm through gently.

Meanwhile, remove the plastic from the gravy and reheat slowly, bringing the sauce to a boil and whisking the fat back into it so that it is semi-emulsified.

To finish the risotto, heat the extra chicken stock until hot. Place a heavy pan on the stove and add the risotto with some of the hot stock and the butter. Take note that the amount of stock suggested is approximate and more should be added only if the risotto becomes dry or thick.

Bring the mixture to a boil and cook for 2-3 minutes or until the rice is tender. When the risotto is cooked, the texture should be a smooth emulsion of stock and butter; the mass should just hold its own weight.

Add the wild mushrooms, chopped chives and parmesan and fold into the rice. Adjust the seasoning, adding the truffle oil a little at a time as required to achieve just an undertone of truffle. Recheck the consistency and seasoning.

Slice the roast chicken portions at a 45 degree angle into 6-7 pieces, keeping the form intact (14).

When all the components are ready, place the greens and onions in the centre of each serving plate. Top with the risotto and lay the sliced chicken on top (15). Add a quenelle of warm leek cream, drizzle the gravy and truffle dressing around the plate and serve.

Chefs' notes
The great thing about this dish is how versatile the components are. The chicken, for example, could be the star of your Sunday lunch, while the risotto could stand alone as a starter or hearty main course.

13

14

15

Barbary Duck, Vanilla-Lime Mash and Jus

When roasting game birds or poultry, the rule of thumb has always been that they must be cooked on the bone to retain their flavour and shape. In this, and most of my other duck recipes, the breast is taken off the bone first to ensure all the fat is rendered down to give a crispy skin. This process also helps time the cooking to perfection, which is normally difficult because the ratio of bone to meat to fat varies from duck to duck. The inclusion of lime and vanilla in this dish works well because they cut through the richness of the bird. To be really decadent, you could quickly roast a piece of foie gras for each person while garnishing the dish and place it on the duck just before serving. SERVES 6

VANILLA SAUCE
3 vanilla beans
25ml/1floz/1½ tbsp corn oil
100g/4oz/1 cup mirepiox
 (see page 159)
75ml/3floz/⅓ cup red wine
25ml/1floz/1½ tbsp port
25ml/1floz/1½ tbsp brandy
2 tsp armagnac
250ml/9floz/1¼ cup lamb
 jus (see page 156)
25ml/1floz/1½ tbsp good
 quality vanilla extract

MASHED POTATO
300g/10½oz Maris Piper or
 other floury potatoes,
 peeled
125ml/4½floz/½ cup
 double (heavy) cream
½ tbsp butter
salt

DUCK
6 Barbary duck breasts
a pinch of duck spice (see
 page 163)

ROAST PARSNIPS
4 large parsnips, peeled
4 tsp olive oil
75g/3oz/¾ stick butter

TO FINISH
200g/7oz spinach, picked
20g/¾oz/1 tbsp butter
3 limes, cut into segments

Thinking ahead The sauce is easiest made the day before and stored in the fridge in an airtight container, that way you have the time to dry out the vanilla beans to use as a garnish. The duck spice can be made 1 day in advance too. The potato purée and lime segments can be prepared up to 2 hours ahead, the potato stored at room temperature and the lime in the fridge. Cook the parsnips in the same pan that you use for the duck so the parsnips take on some of the duck flavour.

FOR THE VANILLA SAUCE Cut the vanilla beans lengthwise with a sharp knife and scrape all the tiny seeds away from the centre. Retain the vanilla seeds for later use (1).

In a saucepan, heat a little oil and cook the mirepoix until light golden brown and a little soft. Add the vanilla beans and cook for 2-3 minutes to extract the flavour. Add all the liquors and bring to a boil, stirring. Pour in the lamb jus and simmer for 45 minutes.

Add the vanilla extract and pour the sauce through a fine strainer into a clean pan. Remove the vanilla beans, wash them off and retain. Add half the vanilla seeds to the sauce, whisking to disperse the seeds evenly.

Either store the sauce overnight in the fridge or cover the pan with plastic wrap and hold at room temperature for up to 1 hour before serving.

If desired, to add an extra touch of style to the dish, cut the vanilla beans in half again lengthwise to give 12 thin strips (2). Leave them to dry in a warm place overnight to use as a garnish for the mashed potato.

FOR THE MASHED POTATO In a saucepan, cover the potatoes with cold salted water and bring to a simmer.

Cook for 20-25 minutes, ensuring the potatoes do not break up in the pan. Meanwhile, in a separate saucepan, simmer the cream until it has reduced in volume by two-thirds. Add the butter and whisk to an emulsion.

Drain the potatoes in a colander, then return to the pan and dry out, expelling as much moisture as possible. Purée the potato using a ricer or sieve. Season to taste, then fold in the cream mixture (3) and the rest of the reserved vanilla seeds. Stir to disperse evenly.

FOR THE DUCK Pat dry the duck breasts if necessary, then trim any sinew and excess fat from the meat side.

Turn the duck breasts so that the flesh side is facing down and, using a sharp knife, score the fat 3mm/⅛in apart, working up the breast and being careful not to cut too far into the breast and expose the meat (4).

Season generously with the duck spice but be careful not to over season. A good guide is to use a little more than you would pepper. Cover and place in the fridge for up to 1 hour to allow the spices to flavour the meat.

FOR THE PARSNIPS Cut the parsnips into batons measuring about 9 x 1cm/3½ x ½in (5) and set aside until ready to complete the dish.

TO COMPLETE Heat a heavy-based pan on the stove over a medium heat. Place the duck breasts in the pan fat-side down and allow the fat to render into the pan, creating a cooking medium for the duck (6). Cook, turning occasionally, for 10-12 minutes ensuring the skin turns golden brown. Remove from the pan and leave to rest for 5-6 minutes in a warm place.

Heat the olive oil in the pan in which you cooked the duck and add the parsnips. Cook until slightly borwned, then add the butter. Reduce the heat and allow the butter to foam

until it is nut coloured (7). Cook in the butter for 8–10 minutes or until the parsnips are just soft to the touch.

Warm the sauce and mashed potatoes in separate pans, adding equal quantities of lime segments to them both. In another hot pan, wilt the spinach in some butter and season to taste.

Place the warmed mashed potato in a piping bag and pipe a mound of it on one side of each plate (8). Drain the spinach well and place a thin line of it down the opposite side of the plate.

Cut each duck breast diagonally to give 2 good strips of meat (9). Place the parsnips on the spinach, then the duck on top of this. Garnish the dish with the sauce and serve.

Chef's notes When using vanilla extract, it is essential that you use extract and not essence as the latter is made mostly from chemicals and contains hardly any vanilla. Using it will spoil this dish.

Rabbit Saddle, Tarragon Tortellini

A mix of sunny Mediterranean and elegant French flavours features in this complex recipe. The use of pasta and cous cous is unusual but works because there is little starch in the finished dish. I like the lightness of cous cous and, while it is often served as a filler in traditional North African meals, here it is a vehicle for the intense taste of tomato. Previously I have accompanied this rolled rabbit saddle with the braised cabbage on page 60. **SERVES 6**

RABBIT

3 long saddles rabbit, livers
    retained
150g/5oz spinach leaves
6 thin slices Parma ham

TORTELLINI

300g/10½oz/1¼ cups
    chicken mousse (see page
    159)
1 tsp wholegrain mustard
1 tsp chopped tarragon
1 batch pasta dough (see
    page 159)

LENTIL SAUCE

30g/1oz/⅛ cup Umbri or
    Puy lentils
3 plum tomatoes, blanched
    and de-seeded
300ml/11floz/1½ cups
    chicken stock (see page
    157)
40g/1½oz/2 tbsp cold
    butter, diced
1 tsp chopped chives
sherry vinegar, to taste

COUS COUS

1 litre/1¾ pints/4½ cups
    tomato juice
1 sprig thyme
1 clove
200g/7oz/1 cup cous cous

LICORICE FOAM

100ml/4floz/½ cup chicken
    stock (see page 157)
150ml/6floz/¾ cup milk
4 tsp cream
20g/¾oz/1 tbsp butter
licorice essence, to taste

TO FINISH

12 small braised shallots (see
    page 160)
100g/3½oz wild mushrooms
    such as black trompette,
    cep, or morels
250g/9oz spinach leaves

Thinking ahead If you have a good relationship with your butcher, he will bone the rabbit for you. Ask for both sides of the saddle to be kept together and all the bones removed. The chicken mousse can be made 1 day in advance along with the pasta and chicken stock. The braised shallots could be made the day before but would benefit from being made the same day.

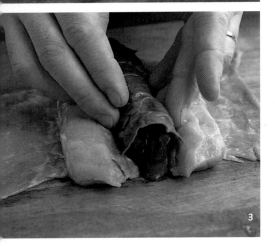

FOR THE RABBIT Split the two natural halves of the rabbit liver with a sharp knife (1), keeping them as whole as possible. Remove any sinew. Wrap the livers in the spinach leaves.

Trim off any excess fat from the belly flaps of the rabbit (2). Lay the spinach-wrapped livers in the cavity (3).

On a 30cm/12in square sheet of foil, lay 2 pieces of the parma ham close together. Place the rabbit saddle with the livers facing upwards on the ham (4). Roll into a sausage shape, twisting the ends of the foil to ensure a tight parcel (5). Repeat with the remaining rabbits and place in the fridge overnight.

FOR THE TORTELLINI Mix the mousse, mustard and tarragon together. Take a small ball of this mixture and wrap it in plastic. In a small pan of gently simmering water, poach the ball of mousse until cooked. Taste to check the seasoning, then adjust as necessary.

Cut the pasta into 6 discs with a pastry cutter. Using a pasta machine, roll them into 13cm/5in circles, turning the pasta 180 degrees through each turn (6). Lay the rolled discs out on a lightly floured surface.

Spoon a heaped teaspoon of mousse onto each pasta disc (7). Fold over the top of the pasta, giving a pasty like shape, and seal the sides with water. Use the pastry cutter to help pack the filling neatly (8), then trim the joined ends, leaving a minimum of 2.5cm/1in pasta dough around the mousse.

Place each parcel in front of you with the curved side facing away from you. Pinch the ends of the parcel together with the forefingers and thumbs of each hand (9). Press together firmly to ensure a secure join (10).

Bring a large pan of water to the boil. Meanwhile, fill a large bowl with cold water and a few ice cubes ready to refresh the cooked pasta.

Place the tortellini in the boiling water for 3 minutes. Remove and refresh in the iced water. The tortellini can then be stored chilled with a little oil drizzled over the top in a container.

FOR THE LENTIL SAUCE In a saucepan, bring a generous quantity of water to the boil ready to blanch the tomatoes. Half-fill a bowl with water and ice cubes to stop the cooking.

Core the tomatoes and score a cross at the rounded end of each. Carefully place the tomatoes into the pan of boiling water and leave them for just 8-10 seconds or until the skin starts to come away from the flesh. Using a perforated spoon, remove immediately and plunge into the iced water.

Cut each tomato lengthwise into quarters and remove the seeds. Lay on paper towel for 30 minutes to dry off the excess moisture.

Meanwhile, in a separate saucepan, cook the lentils in boiling water for 25-30 minutes and drain when tender. Also, place the chicken stock in a saucepan, bring to the boil and simmer until the volume of liquid has reduced to 150ml/5floz/⅔ cup.

Cut the tomato fillets into 1cm/½in dice. Set aside until ready to finish the sauce at serving time.

FOR THE COUS COUS Place the tomato juice, thyme and garlic in a saucepan and bring to the boil. Simmer vigorously until the volume of liquid has reduced by half.

Place the cous cous in a bowl. When the tomato liquid has reduced, pour it over the cous cous and mix well (11). Cover and set aside until the cous cous has absorbed all the liquid. The cous cous can be left like this for up to 1 hour and remain tepid.

FOR THE LICORICE FOAM Place all the ingredients except the licorice essence in a large saucepan and heat just until a slight steam starts to appear. Adjust the seasoning to taste.

Using a whisk or electric hand blender, agitate the sauce to a foam (12) and begin adding the licorice in tiny amounts to ensure you do not overpower the sauce. Bring the sauce back to a foam after each addition of licorice. The sauce can be kept covered for 20 minutes at room temperature.

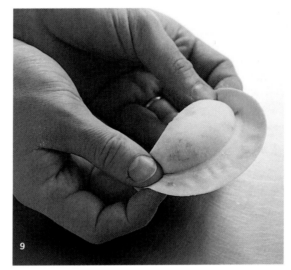

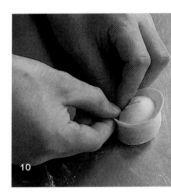

TO COMPLETE Preheat the oven to 180°C/350°F/Gas 4. Place a large pan of water on the stove and bring to the boil ready to reheat the tortellini.

Place the rabbit saddles on a baking tray and roast for 17 minutes, turning after 10 minutes. Meanwhile, warm the shallots in a small pan.

In a frying pan, cook the mushrooms in a little butter and season to taste. Place in a bowl and cover with plastic – they will stay hot for 5-8 minutes next to the stove. In a separate pan, wilt the spinach in a little butter then place it in a bowl, cover, and keep warm.

Ensure the reduced chicken stock is warmed. Remove the rabbit from the oven and rest for 3-4 minutes in the foil. Place the tortellini in the boiling water to heat through 3 minutes.

To finish the sauce, add the butter to the reduced chicken stock and whisk to an emulsion. Add the cooked lentils, tomato and chives, and add salt and pepper to taste. Finish with the sherry vinegar, adding enough so that you can just taste the acid in the background.

Place the cous cous, mushrooms and onions on the serving plates. Squeeze the excess moisture from the spinach and place a mound of it in the corner of each plate (13).

Remove the tortellini from the water and place on rack to drain. Cover with plastic wrap to keep warm. Meanwhile, agitate the licorice sauce to a foam with a whisk or hand blender. Remove the foil from the rabbit and slice each saddle into 4 equal pieces (14).

Lay the sliced rabbit on the cous cous. Place the tortellini on the plate. Garnish the dish with the lentil and licorice sauces and serve.

Chef's notes
If rabbit does not appeal, a crown of chicken such as that used on page 72 can be served instead, using tarragon instead of sorrel. When switching from sorrel butter to tarragon butter, use half the amount of tarragon.

11

12

13

14

Slow Cooked Beef, Rib Meat and Onion Ice Cream

This dish may sound a little unusual, but some will think it a wonderful combination of hot and cold sensations. Others may raise an eyebrow, but it must be tried at least once. The name says 'slow cooked' and this means exactly what it says: meat cooked slowly at a low temperature. The beef never reaches more than 60°C/140°F, which ensures maximum tenderness because the beef's collagen will toughen if cooked above that temperature. SERVES 4

RIB MEAT
50ml/2floz/¼ cup corn oil
400g/14oz rib meat off the
    bone
250g/9oz/1¼ cups mirepoix
    (see page 159)
1 clove garlic
1 sprig thyme
400ml/14floz/1¾ cups
    red wine

300ml/11floz/1⅓ cups lamb
    jus (see page 156)
25ml/1floz/1½ tbsp sherry
    vinegar

FILLET OF BEEF
4 fillet steaks, about
    170g/6oz each
50ml/2floz/¼ cup corn oil
salt and pepper

ONION ICE CREAM
6 onions, peeled
175ml/6floz/¾ cup semi-
    skimmed milk
125ml/4½floz/½ cup cream
1 tsp salt
milled pepper
2 tsp sugar

VEGETABLE GARNISH
8 baby carrots
8 baby leeks

8 baby confit onions (see
    page 160)
350g/12oz/1½ cups potato
    purée (see page 160)

HORSERADISH
EMULSION
50ml/2floz/¼ cup water
50ml/2floz/¼ cup cream
200g/7oz/1¾ sticks butter
½ tbsp freshly grated
    horseradish

Thinking ahead High quality beef is essential for this dish. When buying rib meat, ask for the meat in between the bones of the fore rib or wing rib. The rib meat will need to be cooked the day before. The onion ice cream mixture can also be made 1 day in advance and stored unfrozen in the fridge. The confit onions can be made up to 2 days ahead if desired. The plates used for serving this dish should not be too hot, but above room temperature.

FOR THE RIB MEAT Preheat the oven to 150°C/300°F/Gas 2. Trim any excess fat from the meat. Heat the oil in a heavy casserole and add the rib meat, mirepoix, garlic and thyme. Cook for 5-6 minutes until brown.

Add the wine, bring to the boil and simmer until reduced by half. Add the jus, then cover with foil and cook in the oven for 3-4 hours.

Remove from the oven and leave the meat to cool in the liquor. Remove the ribs and set aside. Strain the sauce into a clean pan and bring it to the boil. Simmer until it has reduced to a thick sauce, but be careful not to over-reduce.

Meanwhile, dice the rib meat into 1cm/½in pieces (1) and add to the sauce. This can be cooled and then kept overnight in the fridge. The flavour of the sauce may need to be adjusted with vinegar to cut through the richness – do not add too much as you want only an undertone of vinegar.

FOR THE BEEF FILLET Preheat the oven to 60°C/140°F/Gas ½. Heat a little oil in a nonstick pan over a high heat. Lightly season the meat and, one by one, quickly (less than 30 seconds) seal the fillets until lightly coloured all over (2). Place on a roasting tray and roast for about 55 minutes, turning halfway through cooking.

FOR THE ICE CREAM Slice the onions and place in a pan with a little water. Place over a very low heat and cook gently for about 1 hour until the onions are soft and starting to brown. Cool slightly, then transfer to a food processor and purée until fine. Weigh out 350g/12oz/1½ cups of the purée.

Heat a little milk in a saucepan and dissolve the sugar in it. Combine with the onion purée and the remaining ice cream ingredients. Chill the mixture in an airtight container if making in advance or proceed as follows.

Churn the onion mixture in an ice cream machine, then transfer to a container and keep frozen until serving.

FOR THE HORSERADISH EMULSION Whisk together all the ingredients in a saucepan, without letting them boil or simmer as the mixture will separate and turn greasy. Keep warm until ready to serve.

FOR THE VEGETABLE GARNISH Peel the carrots and cut into 3cm/1in pieces. Using a small knife, pare the pieces of carrot into barrel shapes. Trim the tops and roots of the baby leeks but do not cut the root right off.

Prepare an ice bath to stop the cooking of the vegetables. In a large pan of boiling salted water, cook the carrots for 6 minutes, then the leeks

for 4 minutes. Remove each batch and leave to cool in the iced water. Drain the vegetables and set aside.

TO COMPLETE In separate pans, heat through the mashed potato and the rib meat and sauce.

Place the blanched vegetables in the horseradish emulsion with the confit onions and warm through (3).

Place a small amount of potato on one side of the plate and add the vegetables. Cut the beef into two pieces per person (4) and place on top of the vegetables. Add the rib meat and drizzle the sauce around the plate. Place a dab of mashed potato on the other side of the plate and sit a scoop of ice cream on top (the potato will keep it from sliding). Serve immediately.

Chef's notes
If you do not have an ice cream machine, you can achieve a similar effect by placing the mixture in the fast-freeze compartment of a domestic freezer and stirring occasionally with a whisk. If the ice cream freezes too hard, remove it from the freezer and stir back to a soft scooping texture. Using a digital probe thermometer would be helpful when testing the cooked temperature of the beef (see page 167).

Roast Rump of Lamb, Flageolet Purée and Balsamic Dressing

In France, roast lamb and flageolet beans are considered perfect partners. The twist to this dish is the sauce, a combination of flavours that not only excites the palate but sharpens the unctuousness of the lamb and offers a subtle sweetness to offset the acid in the tomatoes. The sweet, sour, salty and bitter taste receptors in the tongue are all stimulated, creating an unusual sensation on the palate. SERVES 6

SHALLOT PURÉE
6 large shallots, unpeeled
1 clove garlic
1 sprig thyme
a splash of olive oil

FLAGEOLET PURÉE
225g/8oz/1¼ cups dried
    flageolet beans
1 litre/1¾ pints/4½ cups
    chicken stock (see page
    157)
100g/3½oz smoked back
    bacon or pancetta
    trimmings

½ carrot
1 shallot
½ clove garlic
1 sprig thyme
2 tsp salt

SALSIFY
6 sticks salsify
juice of 1 lemon
50g/2oz/⅓ cup flour
50g/2oz/½ stick butter

FONDANT POTATO
3 medium potatoes,
    preferably Maris Pipers
50ml/2floz/¼ cup corn oil

2 cloves garlic, halved
150g/5oz/1¼ sticks butter
100ml/4floz/½ cup water

BALSAMIC DRESSING
1 clove garlic
½ tsp redcurrant jelly
1 tsp lemon oil (see page
    162)
2 tsp good quality balsamic
    vinegar
½ tsp thyme leaves
6 dried tomato fillets, diced
    (see page 161)
300ml/11floz/1⅓ cups lamb
    jus (see page 156)

LAMB
6 lamb rumps off the bone,
    150–160g/5–5½oz each,
    trimmed
salt and pepper

TO FINISH
200g/7oz spinach leaves
6 cloves garlic confit (see
    page 160)
a few sprigs of chervil

Thinking ahead You will need to soak the beans overnight before cooking, and they can be cooked the day before serving. The fondants need to be made 1 hour before serving to ensure maximum flavour. The lemon oil, stocks and jus can be made well in advance and kept in the freezer. The tomato fillets can be made 3 days in advance. The garlic confit can be made up to 2 days in advance but is best made on the day of serving.

FOR THE SHALLOT PURÉE Heat
the oven to 180°C/350°F/Gas 4. Place
the shallots, garlic, thyme and olive oil
on a 30cm/12in square piece of foil.
Fold over to make a bag and seal the
edges. Place the bag on a baking tray
and place cook for 25–30 minutes until
the shallots are soft and fully cooked
inside. Set aside to cool.

Trim off the skin from the shallots (1).
Discard the rest of the ingredients.
Place the shallots in a food processor
and purée to a smooth pulp. If it is very
runny, place it in a saucepan and cook
until thick, stirring constantly with a
rubber spatula to prevent burning – be
careful to remove all purée from the
corners of the pan while reducing (2).

If making this 1–2 days before
serving, place the reduced purée in
a covered container in the fridge;
alternatively, keep it warm for service.

FOR THE FLAGEOLET PURÉE
Soak the beans overnight. Next day,
rinse in cold water and place in a
saucepan over medium heat with the
stock, bacon, carrot, shallot, garlic and
thyme. Simmer for 20 minutes.

Add the salt and cook the flageolet
for a further 30 minutes until tender.
If the liquid starts to reduce too much
during cooking and no longer covers
the flageolet, top up with filtered water.

Leave the beans to cool in the
cooking liquor. When cold, strain off
and reserve the liquid. Remove and
discard the garlic.

Place the beans and other ingredients
in a food processor and liquidize until
very smooth, adding the retained liquor
if the consistency appears too thick (3).
When the beans are the consistency of
wet mashed potato, either place the
mixture in an airtight container and
store in the fridge overnight, or keep
warm until ready to serve.

FOR THE SALSIFY In a saucepan,
place 1 litre/1¾ pints/4½ cups water.
Squeeze in the lemon juice and whisk
in the flour until it has dissolved. This
is called a blanc. Bring it to the boil,
stirring occasionally, until the liquid
thickens slightly.

Meanwhile, peel the salsify, trim off
any blemishes and cut in half (4). Cook
it in the blanc for 12–15 minutes until
it is just soft in the centre. Allow the
salsify to cool slightly in the cooking
liquid, then remove it and trim into
18 equal pieces (5). Store in a covered
container in the fridge.

FOR THE FONDANT POTATO
Heat the oven to 170°C/325°F/Gas 3.
Peel the potatoes and cut into slabs
approximately 4cm/1½in thick. Using a
round pastry cutter, cut the slabs of
potato into 5cm/2in circles and trim
off the sharp edges (5).

In an ovenproof saucepan, heat the
corn oil over a medium-high heat.
Add the potatoes and garlic and brown
the potatoes on one side, taking care
not to scorch them. Turn the potatoes
over when golden brown and add the
butter, water and seasoning. Bring to a
simmer, then transfer to the oven for
12–15 minutes or until the centre of
the potatoes is soft.

Remove from the oven and leave the
potatoes to soak up the butter for
about 1 hour. If the water in the pan
has evaporated and only butter is left,
top up the pan with hot water.

FOR THE BALSAMIC DRESSING
In a small saucepan, combine all the
ingredients for the balsamic dressing
and bring to simmering point.
Immediately remove from the heat,
cover with plastic wrap and leave to
infuse for 30 minutes before serving.

TO COMPLETE Heat the oven to 180°C/350°F/Gas 4. Place a large frying pan on the stove over a medium-high heat and add the oil.

Season the lamb with salt and pepper and place in the pan 2 at a time, fat-side down. Cook until golden brown on the fatty side, then turn over and seal the meat side (6).

When all the lamb is sealed, place it on a wire rack over a baking sheet and cook in the oven for 12-13 minutes, turning occasionally. Test the lamb for doneness by using the finger and thumb technique (see page 166).

Meanwhile, drain the potatoes and keep warm. Place the confit of garlic in the oven for 3 minutes to heat through.

In a saucepan, reheat the flageolet purée and, in a separate pan, reheat the salsify in a little butter. Check the seasoning of each dish component.

When the lamb is cooked, remove it from the oven and leave to rest in a warm place for 7-10 minutes. While it is resting, place the spinach in a saucepan with a little butter and wilt. Drain well and place it on the serving plates. Top with the fondant potato, shallot purée and confit of garlic.

Warm the dressing through quickly. Spoon the flageolet purée onto the plates and cross it with the salsify. Carve the lamb (7), arrange it on the plate and pour the dressing over, giving each plate an equal serving.

Chef's notes If you have difficulty sourcing the salsify, it can be replaced by celeriac batons cooked in the same way as the parsnips on page 78. In this dish good quality sun-dried tomatoes could be used instead of the home-dried tomato fillets.

Pork Loin, White Beans and Grain Mustard

All the flavours used in this dish are commonly associated with pork, but the various cooking methods and the manner in which each part is finished makes it something special. The flavour extraction is outstanding. The pork loin is initially sealed in hot oil, allowed to cool, then wrapped in plastic and cooked slowly at a very very low temperature for 2 hours ensuring all the flavours and juices are kept in the meat. SERVES 6

FENNEL AND MUSHROOM POWDER
2 tbsp fennel seeds
5 shiitake mushrooms, stems removed

PICKLED-BRAISED FENNEL
2 medium fennel bulbs
4 tsp corn oil
½ carrot, peeled
½ onion, peeled

1 clove garlic, halved
75ml/3floz/⅓ cup white wine vinegar
200ml/7floz/1 cup chicken stock (see page 157)
50g/2oz/½ stick butter

PORK LOIN
1 short loin pork, eye meat only
100ml/4floz/½ cup corn oil
salt and pepper

WHITE BEANS
200g/7oz/1 cup dried cannellini beans, soaked overnight
1 onion, halved
1 clove garlic, split
2 sprigs thyme
1 bay leaf
100ml/4floz/½ cup double (heavy) cream
1 tsp chopped chives
2 tsp wholegrain mustard

TO FINISH
a little red wine jus (see page 163), or glacé chicken stock
12 fresh shiitake mushrooms
50ml/2floz/¼ cup chicken stock (see page 157)
1 small escarole
50g/2oz/½ stick butter
6 cloves garlic confit (see page 160)

Thinking ahead Ask your butcher to prepare the pork for you and cut it in half across the loin. The stocks can be made well in advance and stored in the freezer. The mushroom powder can be made and stored in an airtight container for up to 1 week, or in the freezer for 1 month. The garlic confit can be made up to 2 days in advance if desired but is best done on the day. The pickled braised fennel can be cooked the day before and stored overnight in an airtight container in the fridge. You will need to soak the beans overnight in soft tap or bottled water before cooking.

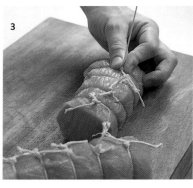

FOR THE FENNEL AND MUSHROOM POWDER Slice the mushrooms very thinly and spread them out on a sheet of parchment paper (1). Place in a microwave oven and cook on medium power for 10 minutes until the mushrooms have shrunk slightly and are crisp but unbrowned. If they are not crisp, return to the microwave and continue cooking until they are. Leave to cool slightly.

Meanwhile, place the fennel seeds in a dry pan and toast over a medium heat for 3-4 minutes, stirring constantly, until fragrant. Remove from the pan and set aside to cool.

Place the mushrooms and fennel seeds in a grinder and mill to a powder the consistency of freshly ground pepper (2). Store in an airtight container for up to 1 week or freeze for 1 month.

FOR THE PICKLED-BRAISED FENNEL Remove the tops and root of the fennel, halve and shred the bulb finely. Heat the oil in a saucepan and

add all the vegetables. Cook them for 5-6 minutes without browning. Add the vinegar and cook for a further 2 minutes, then add the chicken stock and simmer until half the liquid is evaporated and the fennel is tender. Remove and discard the carrot and shallot. If making in advance, transfer the mixture to an airtight container and store in the fridge overnight.

FOR THE PORK LOIN Cut the pork loin in half vertically to give 2 pieces. Take a piece and tie it firmly with kitchen string around the

circumference every 4cm/1½in (3) to ensure the pork keeps its shape during and after cooking. Repeat this process with the other piece.

Heat the oven to 90°C/195°F/Gas ½. Place a large heavy frying pan over a medium-high heat and add the corn oil. Season the pork with salt and pepper, place in the pan and seal to give a light brown colour all over (4).

Remove the pork from the pan and allow to cool slightly. Wrap each in a roasting bag (5).

Lay the wrapped pork on a roasting tray and roast for 1½–2 hours until the meat is slightly firm and has a core temperature of 64°C/147°F when it is measured with a digital probe thermometer. Once cooked, remove the pork from the oven but leave it wrapped in the bag until ready for serving – it will remain warm and moist for 20 minutes in a warm kitchen.

FOR THE WHITE BEANS Drain the soaked beans and place them in a saucepan with the onion, garlic, thyme and bay. Add enough soft tap or bottled water to cover the beans by 5cm/2in and bring to the boil over a high heat. Reduce the heat to a slight simmer and cook for 20 minutes.

Add the salt and continue simmering for a further 15 minutes until the beans are cooked through, topping up the pan with extra water as necessary.

Drain the beans, reserving half the cooking liquid. Pass the cooking liquid through a fine strainer into a clean pan. Add the cream and beans. Bring to a simmer over a medium heat. Cook for about 5 minutes or until the cream slightly thickens. Season to taste.

Cover with plastic wrap and set aside in a warm place for up to 30 minutes – do not allow the sauce to become cold as it may split when reheated.

TO COMPLETE In separate pans, have the beans and fennel warm and ready to finish. When the pork is cooked and has been resting for at least 15 minutes, whisk the butter into the fennel and adjust the seasoning to taste. Warm the jus d'vin or glacé chicken stock in a small saucepan.

Heat 50g/2oz/½ stick of butter in a frying pan over a moderate heat. Cook the cleaned shiitake for 3–4 minutes. Add the chicken stock and escarole and cook until the leaves have wilted (6).

Remove the mixture from the pan and drain. Adjust the seasoning to taste and place it in the centre of the 6 warmed serving plates.

Slice each of the pork loins into 18 x 1cm/⅓in slices (7) and lay them on top of the escarole and mushrooms.

Add the chives and grain mustard to the cream and bean sauce (8) and spoon the mixture around the plate.

Drizzle a little red wine jus or glacé chicken stock over the meat, place the garlic confit on top and serve.

Chef's notes If preferred, this dish could be served with the joint roasted normally for 40–50 minutes in a moderate oven. The white bean recipe is highly versatile and can be used for a number of dishes, including those made with other meats, or dishes featuring robust fish such as turbot and cod. If you would like to purée the white beans, increase the cooking time by 10 minutes, then liquidize them with the cream. White bean purée is particularly delicious with lamb, such as the roast rump on page 93.

Rack of Venison, Buttered Greens and Chocolate Oil

The chocolate oil in this dish is not made using the same techniques I use for other oils, which are colour extraction and flavour infusion. Here, there is little infusion of flavour or colour because the chocolate is already high in fat. Rather, the oil acts as a vehicle for the chocolate taste and as an emulsifier, preventing the chocolate from setting and splitting on the plate. Logistically it would be very difficult to attempt this dish by timing all the components to be completed at the same time. Better is to start cooking the venison only when you are happy with the additional elements. **SERVES 6**

POACHED PEAR

2 large pears, such as
    Comice or Packhams,
    peeled and halved
1 litre/1¾ pints/4½ cups
    stock syrup (see page 164)
3 bay leaves
3 star anise

CELERIAC PURÉE

1 large celeriac, peeled and
    cut into 2.5cm/1in dice
125ml/4floz/½ cup milk
125ml/4floz/½ cup water
75g/3oz/¾ stick butter

CHOCOLATE OIL

100g/4oz bitter chocolate
4 heaped tsp cocoa
4 tsp peppery olive oil
80ml/3floz/⅓ cup corn oil

MERLOT SAUCE

50ml/2floz/¼ cup corn oil
450g/1lb venison trimmings
1 carrot, roughly chopped
½ onion, roughly chopped
2 cloves garlic
½ tsp cracked pepper
1 bay leaf

1 sprig thyme
330ml/12floz/1½ cups
    Merlot wine
1.5 litres/2½ pints/5 cups
    chicken stock (see page
    157)

WILTED GREENS

1 savoy cabbage, stalks
    removed cut into
    1cm/½in strips
250g/9oz spinach leaves
1 escarole, stalks removed
a little butter

RACK OF VENISON

2kg/4lb8oz venison saddle
    loin
50ml/2floz/¼ cup corn oil
salt and pepper

TO GARNISH

a few sprigs of thyme
12 small braised shallots (see
    page 160)

Thinking ahead You will need to ask your butcher to prepare the venison for you. Ask him to tie it and give you the trimmings for the sauce. The chicken stock can be made well in advance and frozen. The stock syrup can be made up to 1 week in advance. The braised shallots can be made 3 days prior to serving. The pears can be made in advance and stored chilled for 2-3 days in the cooking syrup before slicing them for service. The celeriac purée can be made up to 2 days before serving and kept chilled. The merlot sauce can be made 1 day in advance.

FOR THE POACHED PEAR Place all the ingredients in a saucepan and cover with parchment paper. Bring to the boil and simmer for 8-10 minutes or until the pears are tender but still have some firmness when tested with the point of a knife.

Leave the pears to cool and infuse in the cooking liquid, then place in an airtight container and chill until needed, up to 3 days if necessary.

FOR THE CELERIAC PURÉE In a saucepan, cook the chopped celeriac until soft in a mixture of half milk and half water. Drain off all the liquid, then purée the celeriac in a food processor.

When smooth, place the purée in a clean pan and return to the stove. Cook until thick, letting as much moisture evaporate as possible (1). Beat in the butter and adjust the seasoning to taste.

Store chilled in an airtight container for up to 2 days; alternatively, cover with plastic wrap and set aside until serving.

FOR THE CHOCOLATE OIL Combine all the ingredients in a mixing bowl and sit it over a pan of warm, not boiling, water (2). Allow to melt, stirring occasionally, then place in a container and keep warm until serving. The mixture will need to be stirred well just before serving.

FOR THE MERLOT SAUCE In a large saucepan, heat the oil over a medium heat. Working in batches to prevent steaming and give a good colour, cook the venison trimmings until bown. Remove from the pan and set aside in a bowl.

Reduce the heat and, in the same pan. cook the carrots, onion, garlic, bay, pepper and thyme for about 10 minutes or until brown. Return the meat trimmings to the pan and stir well. Raise the heat and, when the pan is quite hot, add the wine. Bring to the boil and boil vigorously until the volume of liquid has reduced by half.

Add the chicken stock, return to the boil, then lower the heat right down and cook the sauce for about 1 hour. Stir it every 10 minutes to prevent sticking and skim off any sediment that rises to the surface.

When the sauce has reduced to about 500ml/18floz/2¼ cups, pour it through a fine strainer into a clean pan. Bring to the boil and simmer again until the volume of liquid has reduced to 200ml/7floz/scant 1 cup, giving a rich plum coloured sauce. At this stage it is ready to serve, or can be kept chilled in a covered container overnight.

FOR THE WILTED GREENS Prepare an ice bath to stop the cabbage cooking. In a large pan of boiling salted water, blanch the cabbage strips for 2-3 minutes, then remove and place in the ice bath. When cool, remove using a slotted spoon and store in a covered container in the fridge.

FOR THE VENISON Heat the oven to 180°C/350°F/Gas 4. If the butcher has not done it for you, trim the

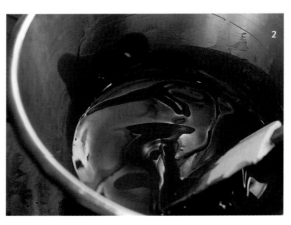

5

6

venison so that the bones rise 5cm/2in above the meat. Tie the venison with kitchen string at intervals along the joint, tying 3 pieces of string between each bone (3).

Place a large heavy frying pan over a high heat, add the corn oil and seal the venison, turning until it is a light golden colour all over Transfer to a roasting tray and cook in the oven for 20–30 minutes until the venison is medium-rare (the residual heat will cook it further). Test for doneness using the finger test (page 166). Remove the meat from the oven and set aside to rest for 10–15 minutes.

TO COMPLETE Have all the components except the venison ready, warm or ready to reheat, then cook the venison (4). Meanwhile, halve the pears and remove the cores and stalks (5). Cut into 3 slices per portion.

In a saucepan, wilt the spinach and escarole in a little butter. Reheat the cabbage by returning it to a pan of boiling water for 1 minute. Drain, then add the cabbage to the wilted spinach and escarole. Finish with a little butter and adjust the seasoning to taste.

Once the venison is rested, warm the braised shallots in the Merlot sauce. Place the greens to one side of the warmed serving plates and the celeriac purée on the other. Place the warmed shallots on top of the greens.

Slice the roast venison into 18 slices, ensuring there is a slice with the bone attached for each plate (7). Layer the venison and sliced pear alternately on top of the greens (8). Garnish the dish with the merlot sauce, chocolate oil and thyme, then serve.

7

8

Chef's notes This can be adapted for rack of lamb by replacing the chocolate oil with thyme oil. The Merlot sauce can be used for other rich meat dishes. Also, do not hesitate to serve the pears as a part of a dessert or breakfast dish.

Desserts

Roast Plums, Honey and Yogurt Ice Cream

This dish combines many taste sensations: sweet-sour plums, warm spices and creamy anglaise. Using bay leaves is unusual in sweet dishes and most people cannot identify the flavour until they're told it is in the mix. However, the anglaise is not too strong and can be served with most desserts – it can even be churned into ice cream. It is a good example of effective flavour building, which involves adding just enough flavour to give an undertone of the taste without overpowering the other components of the dish. The fruit is lovely served for breakfast too. **SERVES 6**

PLUMS

9 ripe plums, halved and
   pitted
3 fresh bay leaves, halved
24 pink peppercorns
3 used vanilla beans, halved
   lengthways
6 star anise
100ml/4floz/½ cup stock
   syrup

HONEY AND YOGURT ICE CREAM

50g/2oz/¼ cup honey
125ml/4floz/½ cup milk
50g/2oz/¼ cup crème
   fraîche
50g/2oz/¼ cup sugar
5 egg yolks
225g/8oz/1 cup plain
   yogurt

BAY ANGLAISE

125ml/4floz/½ cup milk
125ml/4floz/½ cup cream
1 vanilla bean, split and
   seeds scraped out
2 fresh bay leaves
50g/2oz/¼ cup sugar
3 egg yolks

TO FINISH

6 thin slices brioche (see
   page 155)
3 tbsp good quality apricot
   jam

Thinking ahead You will need to make the stock syrup. The ice cream can be made up to 2 days in advance. The anglaise can be made the day before serving – this is not essential, however it will develop a deeper flavour if left overnight. If you wish to make your own brioche for this dish, make it the day before serving, however a good quality store-bought brioche will work fine. Alternatively, a light sponge cake is a good substitute.

FOR THE ICE CREAM Dissolve the honey, milk and crème fraîche in a saucepan over a low heat. Meanwhile, in a large bowl, whisk the sugar and egg yolks until pale (1).

Bring the milk mixture to a quick boil and pour immediately over the yolk mixture, stirring well. Set aside to cool.

When the mixture is cool, add the yogurt (do not add it while hot or the mixture will separate). Churn in an ice cream machine until the mixture holds its own weight. Transfer to the freezer for 4-6 hours to achieve serving consistency. Store for up to 2 days.

FOR THE BAY ANGLAISE Fill a sink half full with cold water ready to stop the cooking of the anglaise – even if the pan is not on the stove, the residual heat can cause it to curdle.

Place the milk, cream, split vanilla bean and bay leaves in a saucepan and bring to a boil. Remove the pan from the heat and cover with plastic wrap. Set aside for 10 minutes so that the bay infuses into the milk mixture (2).

Meanwhile, in a mixing bowl, beat the sugar and egg yolks together until pale in colour. Once the milk has infused, pour it onto the egg mixture, then place in a clean saucepan and return to the heat. Cook, stirring continuously, until the custard is thick enough to coat the back of a spoon (3).

Immediately pour the custard into a clean bowl and sit it in the sink of cold water (4). Leave the custard to cool, then store it covered in the fridge overnight, keeping the vanilla pods and bay in the mixture to impart more flavour to sauce.

FOR THE PLUMS Preheat the oven to 180°C/350°F/Gas 4. Place the plums on a piece of foil measuring 60x30cm/24x12in with the rest of the ingredients and seal to make a pouch (5) ensuring the edges are airtight.

Cook the plums in the oven for 12 minutes. Remove and split open the foil bag, then return it to the oven for a further 5 minutes.

Remove the plums from the oven and allow to cool slightly in the foil. Retain the cooking liquid.

TO COMPLETE Remove the plums from the foil and set aside. Remove the rest of the ingredients from the foil and set them aside, but leave the juice in the bottom of the pouch.

Trim the brioche into neat 7.5cm/3in squares and lightly toast in a toaster.

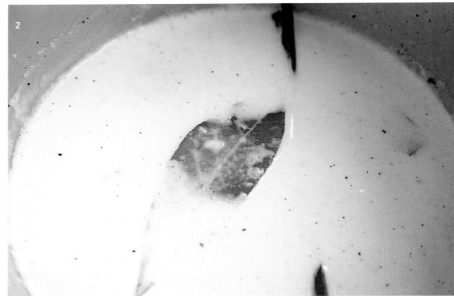

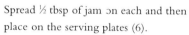

Spread ½ tbsp of jam on each and then place on the serving plates (6).

Using 3 plum halves per portion, place them on top of the brioche. Drizzle the bay anglaise and some of the retained plum cooking liquid around the brioche.

Place half a vanilla bean, 4 peppercorns and half a bay leaf on the plums (7), then top with the ice cream and serve.

Chef's notes This recipe can be adapted for fresh peaches by increasing the time the fruit is cooked in the sealed foil to 20 minutes and the time it is baked with the foil pouch open to 10 minutes.

Chocolate and Griottine Clafoutis

Clafoutis is a famous dessert from the Limousin region close to Perigord in France. It consists of cherries cooked in batter in a buttered dish and served warm with a dusting of icing sugar on top – a sweet Yorkshire pudding if you like. The following recipe moves away from the thick pancake style of batter traditionally used and has a lighter finish. It is great for Sunday lunch with the family, especially on a cold winter day, and is perhaps the easiest recipe in this book. You can vary it by substituting the griottines (cherries bottled in kirsch) with poached pears (see page 101) or some soaked dried apricots that have been flavoured with brandy or liqueur. SERVES 6

CHERRY BATTER
2 eggs
2½ tbsp sugar
180ml/6floz/¾ cup milk
2 tsp kirsch, from the
  griottines
2½ tbsp plain flour

CHOCOLATE BATTER
200g/7oz plain chocolate
100g/4oz/1 stick butter
2 eggs
2 tbsp sugar
2 tsp plain flour
1 tbsp cornflour (cornstarch)

CHOCOLATE SAUCE
(optional)
165g/5½oz/¾ cup sugar
55g/2oz/½ cup cocoa
125ml/4floz/½ cup water

TO FINISH
220g/8oz/2 cups drained
  griottines
icing (confectioners') sugar,
  for dusting

Thinking ahead Top quality chocolate is essential for this dish, so if you need to find a local source, do so in good time. The same is true of the griottines – other forms of preserved cherries such as pie filling, canned or glacé cherries will not do. Good supermarkets sell fine chocolate and griottines these days. Both batters can be made up to 4 days before serving and the chocolate sauce lasts an extraordinarily long time in the fridge.

FOR THE CHERRY BATTER In a
large bowl, beat the eggs and sugar
together until smooth. Add the milk
and kirsch, then sieve in the flour (1).
Mix well, then strain the batter through
a sieve and set aside.

FOR THE CHOCOLATE BATTER
Melt the chocolate and butter in a
bowl placed over a pan of simmering
water on a low heat (2).

  Meanwhile, place the eggs and sugar
in a mixing bowl or a mixer with a
whisk attachment and whisk to a thick
white foam (3). Switch the machine to
the slowest speed, add both flours and
mix for 30-60 seconds.

  Stir the chocolate and butter together
(4), then use a hand whisk to fold this
mixture into the whisked egg mixture,
ensuring total incorporation

  Carefully mix the two batters
together (5) to make one thick batter.
This mixture can be stored in the
fridge for up to 4 days.

FOR THE CHOCOLATE SAUCE
Place all the ingredients in a saucepan
and bring to the boil, stirring to
dissolve. Remove from the heat, cool
and store covered in the fridge until
ready to serve, or for up to 1 month.

TO COMPLETE Preheat the oven
to 180°C/350°F/Gas 4. Lightly, but
thoroughly, butter some sur-la-plat
dishes (white shallow dishes with small
ears on the side). Alternatively use
another ovenproof dish such as a gratin
dish. Place 10-12 griottine cherries in

the base of each dish and divide the
batter between them. Place the dishes
on a baking sheet and bake for 8-10
minutes until just cooked.

  Remove the clafoutis from the oven
and allow it to cool slightly. Dust with
icing sugar and serve, with the chocolate
sauce handed separately if desired.

Chef's notes You could serve ice
cream with this dessert as the contrast of
hot and cold would work wonderfully well.
My suggestion would be pistachio ice
cream. To make that yourself, add
100g/4oz/1 cup of finely chopped roasted
pistachio nuts to the pepper ice cream
recipe (see page 142), and omit the

2

3

4

pepper. Another option is to use fresh
pitted cherries in season in place of the
griottines. In this instance, remember to
add some kirsch or maraschino to the
batter. I would also enjoy parsnips with
this chocolate batter. Cut the parsnips into
cubes and cook them until tender in some
milk, then drain and use as the griottines.

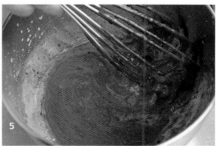

5

Bitter Chocolate Tart, Parsnip Ice Cream

This chocolate tart is very simple to make and easy to serve because you can make it in advance and leave it to reach room temperature. This gives you plenty of time to chat over the main course without being preoccupied with getting the dessert ready. If you have any leftover tart it can be stored in the fridge for up to 2 days and warmed through in the microwave on a low setting for 30 seconds before serving. Parsnips were traditionally used as sweeteners and go remarkably well with chocolate. However, if you would prefer another ice cream with this tart I would suggest choosing vanilla, rum and raisin, or a poire william sorbet. **SERVES 8-12**

PARSNIP ICE CREAM
450g/1lb parsnips, peeled
    and chopped
300ml/11floz/1⅓ cups milk
5 egg yolks
60g/2½oz/⅓ cup sugar
50g/2oz/⅓ cup glucose
    syrup
125g/4½oz/½ cup crème
    fraîche

TART CASE
350g/12oz/3 cups flour
40g/1½oz/⅓ cup cocoa
125g/4½oz/1 heaping cup
    icing (confectioners')
    sugar
200g/7oz/1¾ sticks butter,
    cut into 1cm/½in cubes
zest and juice of 1 orange
1 egg

CHOCOLATE FILLING
3 whole eggs plus 3 egg
    yolks
60g/2½oz/⅓ cup sugar
300g/10½oz/2½ sticks butter
450g/1lb bittersweet
    chocolate
60g/2½oz/¾ cup cocoa

PARSNIP CRISPS
1 large parsnip
ground cumin, for dusting

TO FINISH
cocoa, for dusting

Thinking ahead The ice cream must be made on the day of serving as the sugar content is low and it will set very hard if left in the freezer overnight. The tart case can be made up to a day in advance and kept at room temperature. Be sure to leave the ring on to support the pastry, as it will be needed when the chocolate filling is poured in and cooked.

FOR THE TART CASE Preheat the oven to 180°C/350°F/Gas 4. Place the flour, cocoa and icing sugar in a mixing bowl, add the butter and rub until the mixture resembles breadcrumbs (1).

In a separate bowl, mix the orange zest and juice together with the egg. Add this to the crumb mixture and mix together to form a dough, being careful not to overwork the mixture or the pastry will become tough. Wrap the pastry in plastic and place in the fridge to rest for 30-60 minutes.

Dust a clean work surface with a little flour and roll out the pastry to a circle about 10cm/4in bigger than the circumference of the tart tin, which should be 25 x 4cm/10 x 1½in.

Carefully place the pastry in the ring and gently press it down into the corners, leaving some overhang on the rim (2), which will be trimmed off after the tart has been cooked.

Line the pastry with a double layer of plastic wrap (3), and pour in enough baking beans to fully cover the base and corners of the tart (4).

Bake for 15 minutes, then remove the tart from the oven. Take out the baking beans and plastic and return the pastry to the oven for a further 10 minutes to dry out the base (5).

FOR THE PARSNIP ICE CREAM
Place the chopped parsnips and milk in a saucepan over a medium heat. Bring

to a simmer and cook until soft. Drain, reserving 125ml/4floz/½ cup of the milk. Spread the parsnips out on a tray so that the excess moisture evaporates.

When dry, purée the parsnips until smooth, then place in a kitchen towel or piece of muslin and squeeze out any remaining moisture (6). Set aside.

Place the reserved milk in a saucepan and bring to the boil, taking care not to let it boil over. In a mixing bowl, beat together the egg yolks, sugar and glucose. When the milk has boiled, pour it immediately over the yolk mixture and stir to combine.

Place the crème fraîche in a large stainless steel bowl and set aside.

Return the custard mixture to a clean saucepan and cook slowly over a low heat until it thickens slightly. Do not let the mixture boil or simmer or it will separate, in which case you will have to start over again.

When the custard has thickened enough to coat the back of a spoon (7), pour it over the crème fraîche and mix well. Add the parsnip purée, stir until combined, then churn the mixture in an ice cream machine until firm enough to scoop. Transfer to a clean container and store in the freezer.

FOR THE CHOCOLATE FILLING

Place the whole eggs, yolks and sugar together in a mixing bowl and, using an electric mixer, start whisking them to a sabayon or ribbon stage.

Meanwhile, in a small saucepan, melt the butter and bring to a boil. Remove the pan from the heat and mix in the

5

6

7

chopped chocolate and cocoa, stirring until the chocolate has completely melted into the butter.

Once the egg mixture is light and fluffy (8), fold in the chocolate mixture. Mix well to combine but be sure not to knock the air out of the sabayon (9).

Lower the oven temperature to 150°C/300°F/Gas 2. Pour the chocolate filling into the cooked pastry case and bake for 10 minutes or until the top edge of the chocolate crusts slightly (10). Remove the chocolate tart from the oven, leave it to cool, and then place it in the fridge to chill.

When the tart has chilled, remove it from the fridge, cover lightly with plastic wrap and allow it to come back to room temperature – this will take 2-3 hours. At this stage it is ready to serve, but must be cut into portions only just before serving.

PARSNIP CRISPS Heat some corn oil for deep-frying to 180°C/350°F. Peel the parsnips with a vegetable peeler, discarding the skin, then carry on peeling to give several thin strips of parsnip (11). Place the strips in the hot oil a few at a time (they will cook very

quickly) and fry until golden brown. Remove from the oil using a slotted spoon and drain on kitchen paper. Dust with the cumin while still hot so that the crisps absorb the flavour. These can be made up to 2 hours before service.

TO COMPLETE Run a long sharp knife under hot running water and carefully cut the tart into the required portions (12). Keep any tart not used covered with plastic to prevent drying.

Place the portions on serving plates with the ice cream. Finish with the parsnip crisps and a dusting of cocoa.

White Chocolate Mousse, Raspberry Milkshake

Apart from the milkshake, the constituents of this fun dessert are prepared well in advance, making the serving process itself very easy. Present the milkshake with straws for your guests to use. They will first feel the cold sensation of the raspberry sauce, then the warm milky foam that finishes the drink. Ideally, the milkshake would be fully drunk before the mousse and its accompanying biscotti are eaten. SERVES 6

LEMON BISCOTTI
35g/1½oz/3 tbsp butter
juice and zest of 1 lemon
3 whole eggs plus 2 yolks
300g/10½oz/1½ cups sugar
1 tbsp baking powder
430g/15oz/3 cups cake
　flour
130g/4½oz/1 cup pecans
130g/4½oz/1 cup almonds

WHITE CHOCOLATE MOUSSE
180ml/6floz/¾ cup milk
½ vanilla bean
1½ sheets gelatine
250g/9oz good quality
　white chocolate, chopped
300g/10½oz fresh
　raspberries
250g/9oz/1 cup cream

RASPBERRY MILKSHAKE
(part one)
50ml/2floz/¼ cup raspberry
　coulis (see page 164)
50ml/2floz/¼ cup framboise
　or other raspberry liqueur
(part two)
250ml/9floz/1⅛ cup
　raspberry coulis (see page
　164)
250ml/9floz/1⅛ cup
　skimmed milk

TO FINISH
50ml/2floz/¼ cup chocolate
　sauce (see page 110)
15g/½oz white chocolate,
　shaved or curled
icing (confectioners') sugar,
　for dusting
a few sprigs of mint

Thinking ahead The loaves of lemon biscotti can be made up to 3 weeks in advance and frozen, then defrosted, sliced and rebaked the day before, or on the same day of serving. The raspberry coulis can be made 3 days in advance. The mousse is best made 6-8 hours before serving to ensure maximum flavour from the raspberries; they will start to bleed if left longer. Both stages of the milkshake must be made on the day of serving, preferably just before service, but the chocolate sauce can be made well ahead. The best moulds for the mousse are stainless steel and shaped like drainpipes, about 6.5cm/3in wide and 3.5cm/1½in high. They are readily available from good kitchenware shops.

FOR THE LEMON BISCOTTI

Preheat the oven to 150°C/300°F/Gas 2. Melt the butter in a small pan, then add the grated lemon zest and strained juice.

Place the eggs, yolks and sugar in a mixing bowl and whip lightly to give just a little aeration (1). Sift in the baking powder and flour, then mix using a spatula. Add the chopped pecans and almonds, then the butter and lemon mixture and mix well.

Divide the dough into 3 and shape into ciabatta-like loaves (2). Place on a baking sheet lined with greaseproof paper and cook for 40 minutes until light golden brown, taking care not to over cook or it will be very difficult to slice afterwards. Remove from the oven and leave to cool on a wire rack.

At this point the biscotti loaves can be wrapped and frozen for up to 3 weeks; alternatively, freeze only 2 of the loaves and proceed with the remaining one.

Heat the oven to 180°C/350°F/Gas 4. Thinly slice the loaf into 12 pieces (3).

Place them on a baking sheet and cook for 2–3 minutes or until golden brown. Remove from the oven and cool on a wire rack. Store in an airtight container until needed, for up to 24 hours.

FOR THE CHOCOLATE MOUSSE

Place the milk in a small saucepan over a low heat. Scrape the seeds from the vanilla bean and add them to the milk along with the vanilla bean.

Bring the milk to scalding point, then set aside to infuse for 10 minutes. Meanwhile, soak the gelatine leaves in a

bowl of cold water for 3–4 minutes or until they have softened.

Place the chopped white chocolate in a stainless steel bowl. Reheat the milk slightly, discarding the vanilla bean, then pour 120ml/4floz/½ cup of milk over the chocolate and stir well.

Add the soaked gelatine to the remaining milk (4) and stir until it has completely dissolved. Pour this into the white chocolate mixture. Leave to cool slightly but do not let it become stiff.

Place a layer of raspberries in the base of the moulds (5). Whip the cream

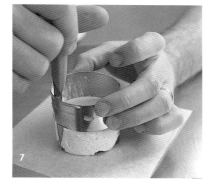

until it just holds its own weight, then fold it into the chocolate mixture, ensuring total incorporation. Whisk the mixture briefly until soft peaks form.

Spoon the mousse into the moulds, making sure there are no air pockets, and smooth off with a palette knife to give a straight edge (6). Place in the fridge to set for up to 3 hours.

FOR THE MILKSHAKE In a small bowl, combine the raspberry coulis and framboise for part one and place in the fridge until ready to serve.

To make part two of the milkshake, place the raspberry coulis in a small saucepan and simmer vigorously, stirring constantly, until the volume of liquid has reduced by half.

Remove the pan from the heat, stir in the skimmed milk and set aside.

TO COMPLETE Using a teaspoon, pour 2 thin strips of chocolate sauce on one side of each serving plate to

decorate. Turn out the mousse using a sharp knife (7) and place it on the opposite side of the plate. Sprinkle the mousse with white chocolate shavings, dust with icing sugar and top with mint. Lay 2 biscotti next to each mousse.

Fill serving glasses about one-third full with the raspberry liqueur mixture. Heat the raspberry milk mixture to 80°C/180°F – do not let it boil. Using a hand blender, whisk the mixture to a froth, then spoon it into the part-filled glasses (8). Place the milkshakes on the serving plates and serve immediately.

Chef's notes The biscotti recipe gives 3 loaves but you only need 12 individual biscuits for this dish. There will be plenty of leftovers, however it is always great to have biscotti around as they go nicely with coffee. The leftover milkshake is a terrific drink on its own straight from the fridge, or it can be served with ice cream.

Citrus Soufflé, Hot Chocolate Ice Cream

This soufflé is one of my favourites. Most soufflé recipes are very sweet but here the citrus syrup and grated zest provide a welcome tartness. Not many restaurants offer soufflés on their menus these days — it's considered a little passé — but at dinner parties a soufflé will always steal the show. Much of the preparation can be done in advance and, contrary to what many people think, the oven door can be opened for a short time while the soufflé is cooking. **SERVES 4**

CITRUS REDUCTION
4 lemons
3 limes
200ml/7floz/1 cup water
300g/10½oz/1½ cups sugar

HOT CHOCOLATE ICE CREAM
250ml/9floz/1 cup cream
250ml/9floz/1 cup milk
3 tbsp drinking chocolate
50g/2oz glucose syrup
85g/3oz/½ cup sugar
6 medium egg yolks

SOUFFLÉ
melted butter, for brushing
75g/3oz/½ cup sugar, plus extra for lining the moulds
210g/7½oz/1 cup crème pâtissière (see page 164)
6 tbsp citrus reduction (see left)
8 medium egg whites
zest of 1 lime

TO FINISH
300ml/11floz/1½ cups skimmed milk
cocoa, for dusting
icing (confectioners') sugar, for dusting

Thinking ahead The citrus reduction can be made up to a week in advance. The crème pâtissière and soufflé base can be made the day before serving, as can the ice cream however it should not be placed in the coffee cups until an hour before service. The soufflé moulds (I use traditional ramekins) should be lined with butter and sugar in advance of making the soufflé as once the mixture is made it should be put straight into the moulds.

FOR THE CITRUS REDUCTION

With a fine grater remove the zest from the lemons and limes. Halve the fruit and squeeze the juice into a saucepan. Add the zest, water and sugar. Cut 2 halves of a lemon in half again and add them to the pan with 2 halves of lime (1). Stir well.

Bring to the boil and continue boiling until the mixture has reduced to a thick syrup and turned golden brown (2). Remove from the heat and strain through a fine sieve. Cool, then store for up to 1 week in an airtight container in the fridge.

FOR THE HOT CHOCOLATE ICE CREAM

In a saucepan, bring the cream and milk to the boil. Remove from the heat and mix in the drinking chocolate, stirring well.

In a mixing bowl, whisk the glucose, sugar and egg yolks until the mixture is smooth and pale yellow (3). Add the chocolate milk to the yolk mixture, stir well, then leave to cool.

Churn the mixture in an ice cream machine until frozen. One hour before service, place the ice cream in coffee cups and store in the freezer until needed.

FOR THE SOUFFLE

Melt a little butter and brush thinly over the inside of the soufflé moulds, leaving no part uncovered (4). Place a handful of sugar in one mould and turn to line it completely with a thin layer of sugar (5). Repeat with the remaining moulds.

Place the crème pâtissière and syrup in a large bowl, mix well and set aside.

When you are nearly ready to serve, heat the oven to 185°C/350°F/Gas 4. In a large bowl, whip the egg whites until soft peaks form. Add the sugar and carry on whisking to give firm peaks.

Gently fold the meringue and cream mixtures together (6), adding the zest. Place in the prepared moulds, ensuring there are no air pockets. Smooth over the top of the soufflés with a palette knife to give a straight edge (7).

TO COMPLETE

Place the soufflés in the oven and cook for 8-9 minutes until they have risen by 5cm/2in and are golden brown on top. When the soufflés have been cooking for 5 minutes, take the ice cream from the freezer and allow to reach serving temperature.

Heat the milk to 80°C/180°F and whisk it with a hand blender until frothy (8). Place the foam on top of the ice cream to give a cappuccino effect (9). Dust lightly with cocoa and place on the serving plates.

Take the soufflés from the oven and quickly dust them with icing sugar. Place the soufflés on the serving plates and serve immediately.

Chef's notes

The most important part of making a soufflé is preparing the moulds – get that wrong and everything else will be wasted.

Panna Cotta with Raspberries

With this dish you can relax during the main course, knowing everything for dessert is ready and all you have to do is arrange it on the plate. It is a very simple recipe. The direct translation of panna cotta is 'cooked cream', but it is hardly cooked at all, just enough to dissolve the gelatine. However, it should not be gelatinous. In my opinion, a true panna cotta should not be turned out of its mould because if it was able to hold its shape under its own weight, it would be too gelatinous, making it a cream jelly rather than panna cotta. SERVES 8

PANNA COTTA
2 leaves gelatine
125g/4½oz/1 heaping cup
  fresh raspberries
560ml/1 pint/2½ cups cream
180ml/6floz/¾ cup milk
90g/3½oz/½ cup sugar
3 vanilla beans

SWEET WINE JELLY
300ml/11floz/1⅓ cups
  sweet wine
55g/2oz/5 tbsp sugar
2 sheets gelatine

LEMON AND
RASPBERRY POWDER
½ lemon, sliced
125g/4½oz/1 heaping cup
  fresh raspberries
icing (confectioners') sugar,
  for dusting

RASPBERRY SORBET
250ml/9floz/1 heaping cup
  raspberry coulis (see page
  164)
120ml/4floz/½ cup stock
  syrup (see page 164)
50ml/2floz/¼ cup framboise
  or other raspberry liqueur

RASPBERRY AND
BLACK PEPPER TUILE
20g/¾oz/1½ tbsp butter
200g/7oz/2 cups icing
  (confectioners') sugar
50g/2oz/⅓ cup plain flour
½ tsp very finely ground
  pepper
2½ tbsp raspberry coulis
  (see page 164)

Thinking ahead Your stock syrup can be made a week in advance. The raspberry coulis can be made 3 days before use. The panna cotta, wine jelly, and powder, can be made the day before serving. It is best if the raspberry sorbet is churned no more than 10 hours before serving. The tuiles can be made 6-8 hours in advance but must be stored in an airtight container.

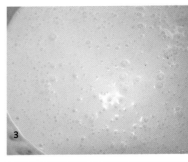

FOR THE PANNA COTTA Place the cream, milk, sugar and the split and scraped vanilla pods in a saucepan and bring to scalding point (1). Remove from the heat and leave to cool and infuse for 30 minutes.

Meanwhile, divide the raspberries between the serving dishes. Prepare an ice-bath and soak the gelatine in a small bowl of cold water for 3-4 minutes.

Squeeze out all the water from the gelatine (2). Stir it into the cream mixture until completely dissolved. Cool the mixture over the ice bath until it starts to slightly thicken and gelatinize (3). This ensures the vanilla seeds are suspended in the mixture and prevents them sinking to the bottom.

Pour the panna cotta into the moulds and refrigerate for at least 3-4 hours.

FOR THE WINE JELLY Soak the gelatine in a bowl of cold water. Meanwhile, in a small saucepan, heat one-third of the sweet wine with the sugar until dissolved. Remove from the heat and allow to cool slightly.

Squeeze the water out of the gelatine and add to the warm wine. Stir until completely dissolved, then add the cold wine and leave until cool but not set.

Divide the wine jelly mixture between the pana cottas, spooning it over the top (4). Refrigerate for at least 30-60 minutes to set.

FOR THE LEMON AND RASPBERRY POWDER Place the raspberries and lemon rind on a plate lined with greaseproof paper (5). Place in a microwave oven and cook on a

low setting for 35-40 minutes. When completely dry (6), place in a grinder and grind to a fine powder. Store in an airtight container until ready for use.

FOR THE RASPBERRY SORBET Mix all ingredients together in a mixing bowl, then churn in an ice cream machine until the mixture achieves a sorbet consistency.

Transfer the sorbet to a clean plastic container. Cover with baking paper, expelling all the air (7) to ensure that very few ice crystals form on top of the sorbet. Freeze for up to 10 hours.

FOR THE RASPBERRY AND PEPPER TUILE In a small pan, melt the butter over a low heat. Meanwhile, sieve the icing sugar, flour and pepper

5

6

7

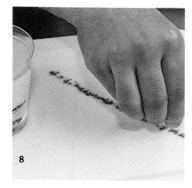

8

into a mixing bowl, then add the raspberry coulis and mix well. Stir in the melted butter and, when combined, place in the fridge for 30–40 minutes until set and ready for use.

Heat the oven to 180°C/350°F/Gas 4. Spread the tuile mixture in 7.5cm/3in rounds on a baking sheet lined with silicone paper. Bake until slightly golden and opaque, about 6–7 minutes. Remove from the oven, leave to cool on the baking tray, then store in an airtight container until ready to serve.

TO COMPLETE Sprinkle a row of the raspberry and lemon powder over each serving plate (8). Place a panna cotta on each. Lay a tuile on each plate, top with a ball of sorbet, then cover with another tuile. Serve immediately.

Chef's notes Care should be taken when making the powder to not burn it in the microwave – you will need to adjust the length of cooking time to suit the power of your oven. When making the panna cotta, a handy tip is to spoon a small amount of the mixture onto a saucer and place it in the fridge for 5-10 minutes to test if it will set properly.

'Rhubarb and Custard'

Rhubarb and custard is a great childhood favourite of mine, reminding me of Sunday afternoons spent with my grandmother. It's real comfort food, just like a thick warm blanket. This dessert utilises that wonderfully simple flavour combination but adds a few modern twists. There are various textures of rhubarb flavoured pudding included, as well as a custard that oozes out of the mousse when you cut into it. With some gelatine added to the custard, the rhubarb compote and ginger sponge could be layered into an excellent trifle. **SERVES 6**

DRIED RHUBARB

1 stalk rhubarb
icing (confectioners') sugar,
    for dusting

RHUBARB COMPOTE

1kg/2lb4oz rhubarb
200ml/7floz/scant 1 cup
    stock syrup (see page 164)
1 sheet gelatine
a squeeze of lemon juice

RHUBARB COULIS

800g/1lb2oz/3¾ cups
    rhubarb compote (see left)
400g/14oz/2¼ cups sugar

RHUBARB AND CUSTARD ICE CREAM

250ml/9floz/1¼ cups cream
250ml/9floz/1¼ cups milk
40g/1½oz/¼ cup glucose
40g/1½oz/¼ cup sugar
6 medium egg yolks
150ml/5floz/scant ⅔ cup
    rhubarb coulis (see above)

GINGER SPONGE

2 eggs
60g/2oz/⅓ cup sugar
½ tsp pickled ginger, chopped
30g/1oz/¼ stick butter, melted
60g/2oz/½ cup plain flour,
    sifted

CUSTARD

300ml/11floz/1⅓ cups milk
1 vanilla bean
3 egg yolks
65g/2½oz/⅓ cup sugar
35g/1½oz/3 tbsp cornflour
    (cornstarch)
100g/4oz/½ cup cream

RHUBARB TUILE

100g/4oz/1 cup icing
    (confectioners') sugar
25g/1oz/¼ cup plain flour
5 tbsp rhubarb coulis (see
    left)
40g/1½oz/1½ tbsp butter,
    melted

RHUBARB MOUSSE

3 leaves gelatine
125ml/4floz/½ cup cream
4 medium egg whites
100g/4oz/⅔ cup sugar
125ml/4floz/½ cup rhubarb
    coulis (see left)

Thinking ahead The moulds needed for this dish are similar to drainpipes and made from stainless steel, measuring 6.5x3.5cm/2½x1½in. They can be bought from any good kitchenware store. If your moulds are out by a little, do not worry as the recipe accommodates slightly varying mould sizes. The dried rhubarb, rhubarb compote and coulis are listed first and must be done in the order given as the strips take a while to dry and the compote is required for other parts of the dish. You need to begin this dish at least one day before serving.

FOR THE DRIED RHUBARB

Using a vegetable peeler, cut the rhubarb stalk into long thin strips and place on a sheet of parchment paper. Dust with icing sugar (1) and leave to dry out in a warm place overnight.

When dry and brittle, transfer the rhubarb strips to an airtight container and store for up to 2 days.

FOR THE RHUBARB COMPOTE

Peel off the hard skin and cut away the splayed end of the rhubarb (2). Cut the stalks into 2.5cm/1in pieces.

In a saucepan, bring the stock syrup to the boil. Add the rhubarb, return to the boil and immediately remove the pan from the heat so that the rhubarb cooks slowly in the residual heat.

When the rhubarb is tender, remove it from the syrup and drain thoroughly, reserving 4 tbsp of the syrup to complete the compote later. Set aside 800g/1lb12oz/3¾ cups of the cooked rhubarb to use in the coulis, and store the remainder of the fruit in an airtight container in the fridge for up to 1 day or until ready to assemble the dessert.

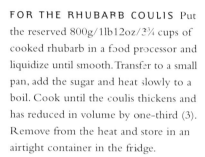

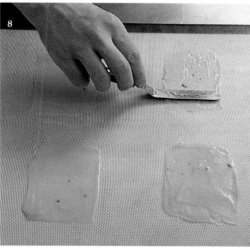

FOR THE RHUBARB COULIS Put the reserved 800g/1lb12oz/2¾ cups of cooked rhubarb in a food processor and liquidize until smooth. Transfer to a small pan, add the sugar and heat slowly to a boil. Cook until the coulis thickens and has reduced in volume by one-third (3). Remove from the heat and store in an airtight container in the fridge.

FOR THE RHUBARB AND CUSTARD ICE CREAM Bring the cream and milk to a boil. Meanwhile, in a mixing bowl, whisk the glucose, sugar and egg yolks until smooth and pale in colour. Add the hot cream to the yolk mixture and mix well, then set aside to cool.

Stir the rhubarb coulis into the egg and cream mixture, then churn in an ice cream machine. When the ice cream has churned, store in the freezer for up to 2 days until ready for use.

FOR THE GINGER SPONGE Heat the oven to 180°C/350°F/Gas 4. Place the eggs and sugar in a mixing bowl and whisk until they reach sabayon stage (4). Add the chopped pickled ginger, then slowly mix in the

melted butter. Gently fold in the flour until it is thoroughly incorporated and there are no lumps in the mixture.

Spread the sponge batter out on a 30cm/12in square baking sheet lined with baking parchment (5). Place another sheet of parchment on top (6) and bake for 6 minutes.

Remove the top sheet of paper and lay it on the worktop. Dust the paper with a little flour and sugar to prevent sticking (7), then place the cooked sponge on top. Remove the second piece of paper and leave to cool.

FOR THE RHUBARB TUILE Sift the icing sugar and flour together into a large bowl. Add the rhubarb coulis and butter and mix to a smooth paste. Chill the batter for 1 hour before use.

Heat the oven to 180°C/350°F/Gas 4. When ready to cook, line a baking sheet with nonstick baking parchment or Silpat. Spread the batter thinly into rectangular tuiles measuring about 10x5cm/4x2in (8).

Bake the tuiles for 6–8 minutes or until golden brown, then remove from the oven. Cool and store in an airtight container for up to 8 hours.

9

FOR THE CUSTARD Put half the milk in a saucepan. Scrape the seeds from the vanilla bean and add the bean and seeds to the pan. Bring to a simmer, then remove from the heat, cover the pan and allow the vanilla and milk to infuse for 10-15 minutes.

Place the egg yolks and sugar in a large mixing bowl and whisk together until the mixture is pale white and slightly fluffy. In a separate mixing bowl, combine the cornflour and the remaining milk and mix to a smooth paste. Pour the hot infused milk onto the cornflour mixture, then stir this into the egg mixture.

Return the custard to a clean pan and bring to the boil slowly, stirring continuously to prevent burning. Remove from the pan, fold in the cream, then leave to cool. The custard

10

11

can be stored in an airtight container for 3-4 hours before use if necessary.

Line 6 indentations of a fairy cup tray or small muffin pan with plastic wrap. Retain 100ml/4floz/½ cup of the custard and set aside for use later.

With the remaining custard, fill the indentations of the cake tray to a depth of about 1cm/½in (9). Place in the freezer for about 2 hours or until the outer edges have firmed up.

FOR THE RHUBARB MOUSSE
Dissolve the gelatine in a little cold water. In a separate mixing bowl, half-whip the cream until it just holds its own weight (10).

Place the egg whites in an electric mixer and beat until stiff peaks form. Add the sugar and continue whisking to a soft meringue.

In a small saucepan, heat about a quarter of the coulis. Squeeze out the

13

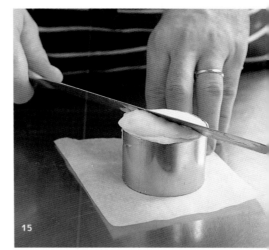

15

14

12

16

gelatine, add it to the pan of coulis and allow the gelatine to dissolve. Pour this onto the meringue and stir to combine.

Using a whisk, fold the cream and flavoured meringue together until thoroughly combined, taking care not to overmix or deflate the mousse (11).

TO COMPLETE Soak the gelatine for the compote in a small bowl of water. Meanwhile, using the drainpipe moulds, cut the sponge into discs and place one in the base of each mould, ensuring a tight fit (12).

Heat the reserved 4 tbsp of syrup, add the soaked gelatine and stir to dissolve. Mix the syrup with the reserved rhubarb compote, adding a squeeze of lemon.

Divide the compote between the moulds, making an even layer on top of the sponge. Place in the fridge to set.

When the rhubarb compote has set, remove the moulds from the fridge and take the tray of custards from the freezer. Spoon a small layer of mousse on top of the compote (13). Then carefully place a frozen custard disc inside each mould, ensuring it does not touch the edges (14).

Fill the moulds up with the rhubarb mousse and level off the top using a palette knife for a smooth finish (15). Place the mousses in the fridge to set for up to 2 hours.

To serve, drizzle the retained custard and rhubarb coulis onto some serving plates. Remove the mousses from the moulds using a thin sharp knife (16) and place on the plates.

Arrange the tuile and ice cream on top of the mousse, finish with the dried rhubarb strips and serve immediately.

Chef's notes This is a complex dish, but if you follow it with the attitude that you are making several small uncomplicated dishes rather than one elaborate dessert, you will find it easy to achieve.

'Strawberry Shortcake', Balsamic Ice Cream

Strawberry shortcake is an American classic that tends to be associated with home cooking. This version is very light and full of flavour. The main change to the traditional recipe is that the shortcake is not heavy but a sablé-style biscuit that melts in the mouth. The mixture given here could also be used to make cookies. Macerating the strawberries draws out their full flavour and adding pepper gives them an intriguing bite. SERVES 6

SHORTCAKE
240g/8½oz/2¼ sticks butter
110g/4oz/⅔ cup sugar, plus
   20g/¾oz/1½ tbsp extra,
   for sprinkling
250g/9oz/2 cups cake flour
30g/1oz/⅓ cup rice flour

BALSAMIC ICE CREAM
250ml/9floz/1 cup balsamic
   vinegar
250ml/9floz/1 cup cream
250ml/9floz/1 cup milk
50g/2oz/⅓ cup glucose
   syrup
85g/3½oz/½ cup sugar
6 medium egg yolks

STRAWBERRIES
500g/1lb2oz ripe
   strawberries
50ml/2floz/¼ cup balsamic
   vinegar
25g/1oz/¼ cup icing
   (confectioners') sugar
milled black pepper

TO FINISH
1 vanilla bean
100ml/4floz/½ cup cream
50g/2oz/½ cup icing
   (confectioners') sugar,
   plus extra for dusting
1 small box wild
   strawberries
100ml/4floz/½ cup
   strawberry coulis (see
   page 164)
a few small sprigs of mint

Thinking ahead The shortcakes can be made a day in advance and kept in an airtight container but for optimum results should be baked fresh on the day of serving. Alternatively, they can be rolled and shaped and frozen uncooked for up to 1 week. The strawberries need to be macerated with the vinegar and pepper 1 hour before serving.

FOR THE SHORTCAKE In a mixing bowl, beat the butter and sugar together until pale and creamy. Add the sieved flour and rice flour and continue beating just until the mixture is combined (1). Wrap the dough in a sheet of plastic and leave it to rest at room temperature for 30 minutes.

Heat the oven to 140°C/275°F/Gas 1. Lightly dust a clean work surface with flour and roll out the dough to 1cm/½in thick. Using a 10cm/4in pastry cutter, cut 12 discs of pastry. Then, using a 2.5cm/1in cutter, cut a hole in the centre of 6 of the discs to hold the ice cream when serving (2).

Place all the shortcake discs onto a baking sheet lined with greaseproof paper and bake for 35-40 minutes or until light golden. When done, remove the shortcakes from the oven and sprinkle them with a little sugar. Transfer to a wire rack and leave to cool to room temperature.

FOR THE BALSAMIC ICE CREAM In a small saucepan, boil the balsamic vinegar vigorously until it has reduced to 100ml/4floz/½ cup in volume. Set aside to cool.

Meanwhile, in a separate pan, bring the cream and milk to a boil, then remove from the heat. In a mixing bowl, whisk the glucose, sugar and egg yolks together until smooth and whitish in colour. Add the cream mixture to the yolk mixture and stir well. Leave to cool, then churn in an ice cream machine.

When the mixture has churned long enough so that it just holds its weight when scooped, add the cooled, reduced balsamic vinegar and continue churning until the ice cream is firm. Store in the freezer until ready for use.

FOR THE STRAWBERRIES Wash and hull the strawberries (3), then chop them into 1cm/½in dice. Lay the fruit on a stainless steel or plastic tray and drizzle the vinegar over evenly (4). Roll the strawberries around in the vinegar to ensure an even coating. Dust

5

evenly with icing sugar, then grind a little pepper over the top – about half the amount you would use if you were seasoning a savoury dish. Leave the fruit for 1 hour to macerate.

TO COMPLETE Split the vanilla bean and use a small sharp knife to scrape out the seeds. In a large bowl, combine the cream, vanilla seeds and icing sugar and whip until the mixture just starts to thicken – it must remain viscous (5).

Place the shortcakes without the holes in the centre of some serving plates. Drain the strawberries in a funnel or strainer to catch some of the juice (6), then add the juice to the coulis.

Divide the strawberries evenly amongst the serving plates, creating a mound on the shortcakes with a slight well in the middle (7). Place the shortcakes with the holes on top of the strawberries, creating a sandwich (8).

Drizzle the coulis and vanilla cream around the shortcakes and decorate with the wild strawberries and mint. Place a quenelle or ball of ice cream in each of the holes on top of the shortcakes and finish with a dusting of icing sugar before serving.

Chef's notes If you do not wish to make the balsamic ice cream, substitute a spoonful of clotted cream per serving.

6

7

8

Tarte Fine of Peach, Pepper Ice Cream

In the tatin of pear (see page 146), I suggest using a commercial puff pastry as a suitable alternative to home-made as the caramelization of the sugar is key to that dish's flavour. This dessert, however, would benefit from the use of home-made pastry. Once you have mastered making puff pastry, which will not take too long, you will be surprised how versatile it is and will begin to wonder if you will ever need to buy commercially produced pastry again. This basic tart recipe could also be made with apricots or pears, and a layer of almond paste (not marzipan), about 25g/1oz rolled out thinly and placed under the fruit would add an interesting flavour and texture. **SERVES 4**

POACHED PEACHES
500ml/18floz/2¼ cups
  water
450g/1lb sugar
2 fresh bay leaves
rind from ½ juiced lemon,
  or a strip of pared rind
3 star anise
6 ripe peaches

PEPPER ICE CREAM
250ml/9floz/1 cup cream
250ml/9floz/1 cup milk
250g/9oz/1 cup glucose
  syrup
135g/4½oz/⅔ cup sugar
6 medium egg yolks
½ tsp freshly ground pepper

TO FINISH
300g/10½oz puff pastry
  (see page 163)
100ml/4floz/½ cup caramel
  sauce (see page 146), made
  using peach juice rather
  than apple juice
icing (confectioners') sugar,
  for dusting

Thinking ahead Ideally the pastry would be made 6 hours in advance however it can be stored for 3 days in the fridge and 2 weeks in the freezer. The caramel sauce can be made the day before. The poaching of the peaches can be done the day before. Peel them and store in an airtight container to save time on the day of serving. The ice cream should be churned 6 hours before serving to allow it time to set and take on the pepper flavour.

FOR THE POACHED PEACHES

In a 2.5 litre/4½ pint/2 quart saucepan, place the sugar and water and bring to a boil. Lower the heat to a simmer and add the bay leaves, lemon rind and star anise. Simmer for 4-5 minutes so that the flavourings infuse into the liquid.

Add the peaches, ensuring that the syrup covers the fruit. Cut a sheet of baking paper into a circle just bigger than the circumference of the pan and place it on top of the contents, pushing down to expel the air (1).

Quickly bring the pan back to the boil and simmer gently for 5-6 minutes. Test the fruit by inserting a knife into a peach – it should be tender but still a little firm. When cooked, leave the fruit to cool in the poaching liquid.

Remove the cooled peaches from the poaching liquid and carefully peel them (2). Store them whole in an airtight container if making well in advance.

Halve the peaches and remove the stones. The stock syrup can be strained and utilised elsewhere in the kitchen, for example in compotes or sorbet.

FOR THE PEPPER ICE CREAM

In a saucepan, bring the cream and milk to a boil, then remove from the heat. In a mixing bowl, combine the glucose, sugar and egg yolks and whisk until smooth and pale yellow (3). Add the milk mixture to the yolk mixture, stir well and leave to cool.

Churn the mixture in an ice cream machine until it just holds its weight when scooped. Add the ground pepper and continue churning until the ice cream is firm (4). Store covered in the freezer until ready for use.

TO COMPLETE On a floured surface, roll out the pastry as thinly as possible to a square 60cm/24in in diameter. Leave to rest for 2-3 minutes otherwise the pastry will become uneven and shrink on cooking. If it is a hot day, cut the pastry into 4 squares and leave it to rest in the fridge.

Cut the rested pastry into 15cm/6in rounds using a tart ring or an upside-down saucer (5).

Halve the peaches and remove the stones. Slice the fruit thinly, keeping the halves together (6).

Place a peach half on one pastry disc, fanning it one-third of the way round, keeping it quite close to the edge (7). Repeat with another two halves to finish the tart, then repeat with the remaining pastry discs and peach halves. Place on a baking tray lined with parchment and chill for 20 minutes.

Heat the oven to 200°C/400°F/Gas 6. Bake the tarts for 15-20 minutes until the bases are crisp. Check the tarts after 10 minutes in the oven and if the bases are starting to turn a little dark, lower the oven temperature.

On serving plates, pour the caramel sauce around close to the rim. Place a warm tart in the centre of each and sit a ball of ice cream on top. Dust with icing sugar and serve immediately.

Chef's notes
Watch the temperature of the pastry while rolling – if it becomes too hot, the butter will melt out of the pastry and your end result will be a greasy tough biscuit. If the peach skin is difficult to peel, which it invariably is if the peaches are not quite ripe, use a small knife to carefully cut the skin away from the fruit.

Tatin of Pear with Roquefort and Pickled Walnut Ice Cream

This is a sublime combination of classic dessert and cheese course, combined to provide a maximum of flavour sensations in the mouth: sweet, creamy, salty, sour and bitter. The traditional method of making tatins can result in undercooked fruit, emulsified butter or burnt pastry. This method which features whole pears will ensure tender fruit with a good flavour that contrasts with the sweetness of the caramel and crisp golden brown pastry. SERVES 6

PASTRY
250g/9oz puff pastry (see
    page 163)

ROQUEFORT AND
PICKLED WALNUT
ICE CREAM
250ml/9floz/1 cup cream
250ml/9floz/1 cup milk

25g/1oz/2 tbsp glucose
    syrup
80g/3oz/scant ½ cup sugar
6 medium egg yolks
4 pickled walnuts, finely
    diced
150g/5oz roquefort cheese,
    finely diced

CARAMEL SAUCE
225g/8oz/1 heaping cup
    sugar
70ml/3floz/6 tbsp water
275ml/10floz/1¼ cups pear
    juice

TATIN OF PEAR
6 large pears, preferably
    Packhams
300g/10½oz/1½ cups sugar
300g/10½oz/2½ sticks
    butter

TO FINISH
12 brandy snaps (see page
    164)
a few sprigs of thyme
sea salt flakes, such as
    Maldon

Thinking ahead If you are making the puff pastry yourself, make it a day in advance. The ice cream mixture can be made the day before but must be churned on the day to ensure a smooth texture. The drainpipe moulds needed for this dish are made from stainless steel and can be bought from any good kitchenware shop. The preferred size is 6.5x3.5 cm/2¾x1½in but if your moulds are out by a little, you can just adjust the pastry. The moulds will need to be lined with tin foil as per the photograph overleaf.

FOR THE PASTRY Roll out the pastry to 3mm/⅛in thick. Cut 6 discs about 1cm/½in bigger than the moulds (1). Prick them all over with a fork, then place on a baking tray and chill until required.

FOR THE ICE CREAM In a saucepan, bring the cream and milk to a boil, then remove from the heat. In a mixing bowl, combine the glucose, sugar and egg yolks and whisk together until smooth and whitish in colour. Add the milk mixture to the yolk mixture and stir well. Allow to cool.

Churn in an ice cream machine until the mixture just holds its weight when scooped. Add the chopped pickled walnuts and roquefort (2) and continue churning until firm. Store in the freezer until ready for use.

FOR THE CARAMEL SAUCE In a saucepan, mix the sugar and water together ensuring no sugar is left on the rim of the pan above the water mark. Place over a high heat and cook to a dark caramel colour (3).

Carefully pour in the pear juice as the caramel will be very hot and bubble vigorously (4). Bring the

mixture to a simmer and cook for 2–3 minutes. Remove from the heat, leave to cool, then place in the fridge to become more viscous.

FOR THE TATIN Preheat the oven to 175°C/325°F/Gas 3. Shape a piece of kitchen foil around the bottom of each mould to form a base (5).

Place a dry heavy pan over a medium-low heat and leave until hot. Meanwhile, peel the pears and trim to fit into the mould, leaving a small gap between the mould and pear (6).

Pour the sugar into the hot pan and allow to caramelize until light brown, stirring occasionally to avoid burning. When the colour has been achieved, pour the caramel into the moulds (7).

Divide the butter between the moulds, putting it on top of the caramel. Place the pears in the mould and bake for 20 minutes – you will start to see the caramel bubble at the sides after 10 minutes.

Remove from the oven and place the pastry lid on top, ensuring it is tucked in at the sides. Cook for a further 15–20 minutes until golden brown.

Remove the tatins from the oven and leave to rest for 2–3 minutes. Carefully

turn out, remembering that the caramel is extremely hot (8). Cool a little before serving. Another way of removing the tart from the moulds is to remove the pastry, then the pear, and reposition it back into the pastry.

TO COMPLETE Drizzle the caramel sauce around the serving plates. Place the cooked tatins to one side of each plate, then place a brandy snap on the other side. Top the brandy snap with a scoop of ice cream and sandwich with the remaining brandy snaps. Decorate with flakes of sea salt and thyme leaves and serve the dessert immediately.

Chef's notes
This recipe works well made into one large tart, in which case the mould would be a 15-20cm/6-8in flan ring lined with foil. Although the method remains almost the same, the pastry may take 3-5 minutes longer to cook.

Foundations

Your daily bread

There are few things in the world as satisfying as good bread and it has been a staple food in many countries for thousands of years. The origins of bread, like most culinary customs, are obscure but many historians believe a form of bread was developed around 9000BC. It was not bread as we know it today, but a thick porridge mixture cooked on hot stones to form cakes, like flat bread or pancakes.

About raised bread we can be a little more exact: archaeological evidence suggests it was developed in Egypt around 4000BC when a piece of old dough was left unbaked and subsequently fermented thanks to airborne yeasts landing on the unbaked dough. This revolutionised the way bread was made. The reaction that took place was very simple. The yeast transformed the starch in the flour into sugar and then into carbon dioxide. The carbon dioxide became trapped, creating air pockets that caused the dough to rise and, when baked, became fixed. With its density lightened, the bread became more palatable. This early form of raising agent was unpredictable, inconsistent and utilized wild yeasts, yet even today some of the best bakeries around the world use fermented dough to make their bread. It is the main raising agent used in the following recipes and, if handled correctly, can be one of the most rewarding, producing bread with satisfying depth and a unique sour taste.

At Lords of the Manor we get through about 8kg/18lb of bread a day, which is a lot for a restaurant of this size. We only make loaves because they can develop a deeper crust than rolls and the core stays moister. We also serve the bread cold because it tastes better. I tend not to encourage eating a lot of bread at dinner, especially if guests are having the tasting menu, because I want them to have room to enjoy the last three courses.

For dinner parties it is best if the bread is baked that day. A couple of hours before you sit down to eat, put the bread in the oven again at a moderate heat for 10-15 minutes to firm up the crust, then take it out and leave it to cool. Slice the loaf and cover it with a damp tea towel to prevent it drying out.

FLOUR White flour is milled from the endosperm of the wheat berry after the husk or bran is removed. Depending on the blend of wheats from which it is milled, these flours may be weak (soft), medium or strong (hard). Strong flour is typically used for breadmaking as it has a high gluten content. Wholemeal, wholewheat and malted flours are a blend of flours commonly known as brown flours. As long as they are labelled strong, they are suitable for making brown bread. Both yield good results but I prefer using malted flour for my brown bread as it gives a moister finish.

SALT Bread would taste insipid without salt, but in addition salt has other properties that help produce a good loaf. It acts as a stabilizer by strengthening the gluten in the dough, improves the colour of the crust, prolongs freshness, and retards fermentation of the yeast. This last factor is important. When making bread you must ensure the salt and yeast do not come in close contact with each other. The concentration of salt in the dough is tolerated by the yeast only providing they are added separately. In the following recipes the salt is added two-thirds of the way into the dough making process.

YEAST This is the agent responsible for the fermentation of the dough. The following recipes use fresh yeast as well as the yeast present in the fermentè, however it is a simple process. By adding the fermented dough, the bread takes on a whole new depth of flavour, with a slight sourness, and the amount of fresh yeast used can be kept to a minimum.

Fresh yeast must be kept in the refrigerator – 4°C/39°F is ideal. It must also be covered to prevent drying, but not too tightly as it is a living bacteria and needs air to breathe. You can substitute dried yeast for fresh, but use half the amount specified in the recipe. It will need to be reconstituted in some of the liquid in the bread recipe. The liquid should be just above blood temperature, no hotter.

WATER The temperature of the water used in breadmaking is crucial. Yeast starts to deteriorate, losing its rising properties, above 50°C/122°F, so water above this temperature can play a significant part in producing a poor dough. Be aware that dough made with hard water will take a little longer to rise.

Summary of the Bread Making Process

DOUGH MAKING All the ingredients must be weighed out before making the dough, whether you are making it by hand or using a machine. A good sturdy mixer with a dough hook attachment is the preferable choice. During mixing, the dough is first formed and then developed. This second stage is essential to the process as during it the gluten is stretched and absorbs the moisture in the dough, giving a good voluminous bread. However it does take substantial time and physical effort if you are not using a machine.

PROVING The dough is now covered to prevent a skin forming and set aside at the temperature of the room in which it was made, not somewhere warm as most people seem to think. When the dough has risen to approximately two-thirds of its original volume, press a finger into the dough. It should give slightly and return halfway to its original form. If the dough collapses when pressed, this indicates an overproved dough in which the yeast has become exhausted.

KNOCKING BACK After the initial proving or rising, the dough should be knocked back – that is, kneaded 2-3 minutes to expel the gas in the bread. Push the dough away from you using the palms of both hands, then pull it back towards you using your fingertips. Continue pushing and pulling with a constant, rhythmic action until the dough feels relaxed.

SHAPING The bread is then shaped into loaves or rolls. I prefer loaves as their longer cooking time helps the bread develop a good crust. To make loaves, weigh the dough into 400-600g/1-1¾lb portions and form them into rounds (or cylinders for placing in bread tins). Alternatively, to make rolls, weigh the dough out into 30-40g/1-1½oz portions. Place the molded dough on a baking sheet lined with baking parchment, or in a bread tin, and cover with a thin damp towel. Leave the dough to prove again until it has risen by around two-thirds and the texture is the same as that achieved during the first proving.

BAKING Remove the towel and dust the dough with flour, rock salt or poppy seeds – whatever you prefer. If using a domestic oven, set it to the hottest temperature; commercial ovens should be set to 240°C/450°F. Place the risen dough in the oven and sprinkle a little water on the bottom of the oven before closing the door – this will give a great crust to the bread. To test for doneness once baked, tap the bottom of the loaf: you should hear a distinct hollow sound, not a dull thud.

FREEZING If you want to freeze the bread (I don't recommend it), place it in the freezer immediately after it has cooled as bread rapidly becomes stale once it is cold.

Fermenté

MAKES 450G/1LB

170ml/6floz/¾ cup fruit juice with a
   high sugar content, such as pineapple,
   pear or grapefruit
280g/10oz/2 cups white bread flour
15g/½oz/1 tbsp yeast

About a week before you plan to bake
your bread, place the fruit juice in a
container and set aside in a warm place
to ferment for 3-4 days.

When the fruit juice has fermented,
place all the ingredients in a food mixer
and mix with a dough hook on low
speed for 6-8 minutes or until a smooth
silky dough has been achieved.

Set the dough aside in a warm place
for 1 day, after which it will be ready to
use and will last up to 3 days.

White Bread

MAKES 15 ROLLS/1 LOAF

10g/½oz/1 tbsp fresh yeast
250g/9oz/1¾ cups white bread flour
75g/3oz/⅔ cup fermenté (see above)
150ml/5floz/⅔ cup water
1 tsp salt

Dissolve the yeast in the water. In a food
mixer with dough hook, place the flour
and fermenté. Pour in the yeasty water
and mix to a solid dough. Mix on low
speed for 4 minutes. Add the salt, then
mix on medium for another 2 minutes.

Remove the dough from the mixer
and place in a bowl. Cover with a damp
towel and leave until the dough has
risen by two-thirds of its original size.

Heat the oven to 250°C/485°F/Gas 10
or the hottest temperature available.
Knock back the dough and shape as
desired. Place it on a baking tray lined
with parchment. Cover with a damp
towel and leave until the dough has
risen by two-thirds.

Bake immediately for 15-20 minutes
for rolls and 40-45 minutes for loaves.
(Commercial ovens will only take 8-12
minutes for rolls and 20-25 minutes for
loaves.) Allow to cool before serving.

Brown Bread

MAKES 20 ROLLS/1 LOAF

15g/½oz/1 tbsp fresh yeast
335g/11½oz multigrain bread flour
   such as Granary (1 cup white
   bread flour + 1 cup stoneground
   wholewheat flour + ⅓ cup
   wholewheat flakes)
165g/5½oz/1 cup fermenté (see left)
15g/½oz/1 tbsp butter
185ml/6½floz/¾ cup water
2½ tsp salt

Dissolve the yeast in the water. In a
food mixer with dough hook, place
the flour, fermenté and butter. Pour in
the yeasty water and mix to a solid
dough. Mix on low for 4 minutes. Add
the salt, then mix on medium speed
for a further 2 minutes.

Remove the dough from the mixer
and place in a bowl. Cover with a damp
towel and leave until the dough has
risen by two-thirds of its original size.

Heat the oven to 250°C/485°F/Gas 10
or the hottest temperature available.

Knock back the dough and shape as
desired. Place on a baking tray lined
with parchment, cover with a damp
towel and leave until the dough has
risen by two-thirds.

Bake immediately for 15-20 minutes
for rolls and 40-45 minutes for loaves.
(Commercial ovens will only take 8-12
minutes for rolls and 20-25 minutes for
loaves.) Allow to cool before serving.

Pickled Walnut
and Raisin Bread

MAKES 1 LOAF

10g/½oz/2 tsp fresh yeast
1 tsp sugar
125g/4½oz/1 cup wholemeal or
   malted (wholewheat) bread flour
125g/4½oz/1 cup white bread flour
100g/4oz/¾ cup fermenté (see left)
10g/½oz/2 tsp butter
110ml/4floz/½ cup water
10g/½oz/2 tsp salt
2 tsp semi-dried raisins
2 tsp chopped pickled walnuts

Dissolve the yeast and sugar in the
water. In a food mixer with dough
hook attachment, place both flours, the
fermenté and butter. Pour in the yeasty
water and mix to a solid dough. Mix on
low for 4 minutes. Add the salt, then
mix on medium speed for 1 minute.
Add the chopped raisins and walnuts
and mix to ensure even distribution.

Remove the dough from the mixer,
place in a bowl and cover with a damp
towel. Leave until the dough has risen
by two-thirds its original size.

Heat the oven to 250°C/485°F/Gas 10 or the hottest temperature available. Knock back the dough and shape it into 1 large loaf or 2 small ones. Place on a baking tray lined with parchment, cover with a damp towel and leave until the dough has risen by two-thirds.

Bake immediately for 40-45 minutes (commercial ovens 20-25 minutes). Remove the dough from the oven and allow to cool before serving or slicing.

Potato and Yogurt Bread

MAKES 1 LOAF

10g/½oz/2 tsp fresh yeast
35ml/1½floz/2½ tbsp water
70g/2½oz/⅓ cup plain yogurt
35ml/1½floz/2½ tbsp milk
250g/9oz/2 cups white bread flour
60g/2oz fermenté (see left)
70g/2½oz/⅓ cup warm, dry mashed
    potato
2 tsp salt

Dissolve the yeast in the water, then add the yogurt and milk. In a food mixer with dough hook attachment, place the flour, fermenté and mashed potato. Pour in the yeast mixture and mix to a solid dough. Mix on low for 6 minutes. Add the salt, then mix on medium speed for a further 3 minutes.

Place the dough in a bowl, cover with a damp towel and leave until the dough has risen by half its original size.

Heat the oven to 250°C/485°F/Gas 10 or the hottest temperature available. Knock back the dough and shape it into 1 large loaf or 2 small ones. Place on a baking tray lined with parchment, cover with a damp towel and leave until it has risen by two-thirds its original size.

Bake immediately for 40-45 minutes (commercial ovens 20-25 minutes). Allow to cool before serving or slicing.

Roast Onion and Pumpkin Bread

MAKES 1 LOAF

10g/½oz/2 tsp fresh yeast
75ml/3floz/5 tbsp water
165g/5½oz/1 heaping cup wholemeal
    or malted (wholewheat) flour
125g/4½oz/1 cup white bread flour
100g/4oz fermenté (see left)
40g/1½oz roasted onions (see page
    160)
30g/1oz/2 tbsp pumpkin purée (see
    page 161)
½ carrot, grated
2 tsp salt

Dissolve the yeast in the water. In a food mixer with dough hook attachment, place the flours, fermenté, roast onions, pumpkin purée and grated carrot. Pour in the yeasty water and mix to a solid dough. Mix on low for 4 minutes. Add the salt, then turn the speed to medium and mix for a further 1 minute.

Place the dough in a bowl, cover with a damp towel and leave until the dough has risen by two-thirds its original size.

Heat the oven to 250°C/485°F/Gas 10 or the hottest temperature available. Knock back the dough and shape it into 1 large loaf or 2 small ones. Place on a baking tray lined with parchment, cover with a damp towel and leave until it has risen by two-thirds its original size.

Bake immediately for 40-45 minutes (commercial ovens 20-25 minutes). Allow to cool before serving or slicing.

Brioche

MAKES 1 LOAF

10g/½oz/2 tsp fresh yeast
20g/¾ oz/2 tbsp sugar
40ml/1½floz/3 tbsp warm water
3 medium plus 2 large eggs
250g/9oz/2 cups white bread flour
125g/4½oz/9 tbsp butter, cubed
1 tsp salt

Dissolve the yeast and sugar in the water. In a small bowl, lightly beat the eggs. In a food mixer fitted with a dough hook, place the flour. Add the yeasty water and mix for 1-2 minutes on a low speed.

Gradually add the eggs and salt. Mix for 8-10 minutes until the dough is silky. Add the butter a little at a time, mixing until the dough is silky again before adding more. Place the dough in a bowl, cover with plastic and chill overnight.

Next day, heat the oven to 250°C/485°F/Gas 10 or the hottest temperature available. Working on a floured surface, divide the dough into 50g/2oz balls and place in a well-buttered loaf tin. Place a damp towel over the tin and leave until the dough has doubled in size.

Bake for 8-10 minutes, then reduce the heat to 180°C/350°F/Gas 4 and cook for a further 10 minutes. Cool on a wire rack. Wrap the brioche in plastic film to store. Freeze for up to 2 weeks.

Stock and Nages

If you have never used home made stock in your cooking, try it and you will be amazed by the difference. For sheer depth of flavour there is certainly no substitute. The results are greater than the sum of the parts, so the small effort you make will be well worth it, especially as stock plays an important role in so many dishes.

My stocks cook for a long time – double the time than in most other professional kitchens. The reason is simple: they are like infusions. The flavours of the bones and other ingredients infuse into the liquid gently instead of being aggressively dragged out by boiling, which breaks down the vegetables and emulsifies the particles and impurities in the bones, yielding a cloudy finish. Once this has happened the stock will not return to a clear state.

Please remember that the stockpot is not a garbage disposal or culinary washing machine. Stock is the foundation of cuisine and needs to be treated with respect. A good idea is to make a large batch and freeze it in ice cube bags or trays for easy use as and when required. Alternatively, reduce your finished stock by half before freezing it in ice cube trays. On defrosting, reconstitute it with an equal quantity of water. This will help save storage space in the freezer. For more detailed information on stock making, see the Science and Methodology section (page 168).

Lamb Jus

MAKES 1 LITRE/1¾ PINTS/1 QUART

2.5kg/5lb10oz lamb bones, chopped into 5-7.5cm/2-3in pieces (ask the butcher to do this for you)
1kg/2lb4oz veal bones, chopped into 5-7.5cm/2-3in pieces (again, ask the butcher)
2 white onions, peeled
2 large carrots, peeled
1 stick celery
1 leeks
1 tbsp tomato paste
500ml/18floz/2¼ cups red wine
2 sprigs thyme
6 cloves garlic
2 fresh bay leaves
8 litres/14 pints/7½ quarts cold water

Heat the oven to 170°C/325°F/Gas 3. Place the lamb and veal bones on a baking tray and roast for 40-50 minutes, turning every 20 minutes, until dark golden brown. Drain the bones in a colander and place the roasting tray on the stovetop. Add a little fat from the bones if necessary to provide enough for sweating the vegetables.

Add the vegetables and tomato paste to the roasting tray and sweat until all the vegetables are well coloured. Using a wooden spoon, scrape up as much sediment as possible from the bottom of the roasting tray.

Pour in the red wine and simmer until the volume of liquid has reduced by half. Transfer the contents of the baking tray to a large pot. Add the bones and the remaining ingredients. Bring to a simmer and skim.

Turn the heat off and allow the bones and vegetables to sink to the bottom of the pot. Then turn the heat back on and bring the stock to just under simmering point – there should be no or little movement in the pot.

Leave to cook over the lowest possible heat for 18 hours, skimming frequently. If it starts to boil, move the pot to one side of the stove so that the temperature stays around 65°C/149°F.

Pass the mixture through a fine sieve into a clean pan. Boil rapidly until the volume of liquid has reduced to about 1 litre/1¾ pints/1 quart.

USES Primarily used for red meat dishes although lamb jus appears in some of this book's fish recipes. It is a good building block for other sauces.
FLAVOUR Rich yet delicate meat taste that can readily be used as a vehicle for other flavours. I use it in meat sauces instead of veal reduction, which can have a gelatinous flavour.
STORAGE Can be stored for up to 5 days if well chilled and can be frozen for up to 1 month.

Chicken Stock

MAKES 2 LITRES/3½ PINTS/2 QUARTS

2.5kg/5lb10oz chicken carcasses
   and wings
2 onions, peeled
3 carrots, peeled
5 cloves garlic
1 leek, trimmed
3 sticks celery
2 bay leaves
3 sprigs thyme
15 whole white peppercorns
5 litres/8¾ pints/4½ quarts cold water

Remove any excess fat from the chicken carcasses and wash thoroughly under cold running water. Place in a stockpot with the remaining ingredients and bring to a simmer. Skim immediately, then turn the heat off and allow the bones and vegetables to sink to the bottom of the pot.

Turn the stock back on, skim again and bring it to just under simmering point – there should be as little movement in the pot as possible.

Cook the stock over a very low heat for 12 hours, skimming frequently.

Pass the stock through a fine sieve into a clean pan, discarding the solids. Bring to the boil and reduce until the volume is about 2 litres/3½ pints/2 quarts.

USES In soups, sauces and for braising white meats. It can also be used to cook and finish risotto, but if the stock is very strong it may overpower the risotto's principal ingredient.
FLAVOUR The strength of flavour is determined by how much the basic stock is reduced. Be aware that reducing it too much can make the stock very salty. The end result should be a clear amber liquid with a rich clean taste.
STORAGE Up to 1 week in the fridge, or up to 1 month in the freezer.

Fish Stock

MAKES 1 LITRE/1¼ PINTS/2 QUARTS

1.5kg/3lb6oz fish bones, preferably
   turbot, sole and brill, no heads or roe
50ml/2floz/¼ cup olive oil
1 onion, finely chopped
1 leek, finely chopped
1 stick celery, finely chopped
½ fennel bulb, finely chopped
5 parsley stalks
5 sprigs thyme
6 white peppercorns
1 lemon, finely sliced
350ml/12floz/1½ cups dry white wine
2 litres/3½ pints/2 quarts cold water

Wash the fish bones and leave to soak in cold water for 1 hour. Drain well.

Heat the olive oil in a stockpot. Add the vegetables and sweat for 3 minutes. Add the bones and sweat 3 minutes.

Pour in the wine and water, bring to a simmer and skim. Add the herbs, peppercorns and lemon then switch off the heat. Cover the pot with plastic film and leave to infuse for 25 minutes.

Strain the liquid into another pan and simmer until reduced by half, skimming frequently.

USES Essential in fish soups for depth of flavour and aroma. It can also be used in sauces or as court bouillon.
FLAVOUR Made correctly, it should taste very fragrant with undertones of fish and herbs and smell fresh, not fishy.
STORAGE Up to 5 days in the fridge, or frozen for up to 1 month.

Shellfish Nage

MAKES 2 LITRES/3½ PINTS/2 QUARTS

50ml/2floz/¼ cup olive oil
500g/1lb2oz unshelled prawns
1kg/2lb4oz crab body, roughly smashed
2 carrots, chopped
1 onion, chopped
1 stick celery, chopped
½ fennel bulb, chopped
2 cloves garlic
2 star anise
3 tbsp tomato paste
200ml/7floz/scant 1 cup dry white wine
2 litres/3½ pints/2 quarts cold water
500ml/18floz/2¼ cups fish stock (left)
5 sprigs parsley
5 sprigs thyme
1 bay leaf

Place a stockpot over a medium heat and heat the oil. Add the whole prawns and crab body and sweat for 8 minutes. Add the vegetables, garlic and tomato paste and continue sweating for a further 8 minutes.

Pour in the wine, bring to the boil and simmer until reduced by half. Then add the water, stock, star anise and herbs. Bring to a simmer and skim. Cook for 30 minutes, skimming frequently.

Strain the liquid through a fine sieve, being careful not to force the solids. Leave the nage to cool then chill and use as required.

USES Shellfish nage can be used in sauces, soups and risottos. In this book we make a frothed sauce that is simply a mixture of reduced nage, cream, butter, milk and seasoning.
FLAVOUR Light and fragrant, with a hint of aromatic spices and herbs. It gives an excellent flavour to all types of fish dishes and sauces.
STORAGE Store shellfish nage for up to 3 days in a airtight container in the fridge, or freeze for up to 1 month.

Vegetable Nage
MAKES 2 LITRES/3½ PINTS/2 QUARTS
3 onions, chopped
2 sticks celery, chopped
2 leeks, chopped
4 carrots, peeled and chopped
1 bulb garlic, halved horizontally
10 white peppercorns
10 pink peppercorns
3 star anise

2 sprigs thyme
2 sprigs parsley
2 sprigs chervil
2 sprigs tarragon
200ml/7floz/scant 1 cup dry white white wine
2 litres/3½ pints/2 quarts cold water

Place all the ingredients in a stockpot, bring to the boil, then lower the heat and simmer for 25 minutes. Turn off the heat and cover the pan with plastic film. Leave to infuse for 1 hour.

Pour the contents of the stockpot into a clean container, cover and leave in the fridge for 24 hours to infuse.

Next day, strain the nage and discard the solids before use or further storage.

USES Vegetable nage is very good for soups and sauces, especially when your guests are vegetarians.
FLAVOUR The flavour you capture in this recipe comes primarily from the 24-hour infusion that takes place after cooking the stock. Once left to infuse the nage will have a clean and distinct vegetable flavour, with undertones of wine, herbs and spices.
STORAGE Store in the fridge for up to 1 week in an airtight container, or freeze for up to 1 month.

Mushroom Nage
MAKES 1¾ LITRES/3 PINTS/1¾ QUARTS
50ml/2floz/¼ cup olive oil
250g/9oz large flat cap mushrooms
1 stick celery, chopped
1 leek, chopped

3 cloves garlic, halved
5 white peppercorns
1 sprig thyme
1 sprig parsley
1 sprig chervil
2 sprigs tarragon
150ml/5floz/⅔ cup dry white wine
2 litres/3½ pints/2 quarts cold water
75g/3oz/3 cups dried ceps
50g/2oz/2 cups dried morels

In a stockpot, heat the olive oil over a moderate heat, then add all of the vegetables except the dried mushrooms (they will make the nage bitter if added now) and sweat for 8 minutes.

Pour in the wine and water and add the herbs. Bring to a simmer, skim, then continue cooking for 30 minutes, skimming frequently.

Remove the stock from the heat and add the dried mushrooms. Leave the mixture to cool but do not strain it. When cool, cover and place in the fridge to infuse for 24 hours.

Next day, strain and discard the solids from the nage before use or storage.

USES Mushroom nage has a number of uses, including soups, sauces, risotto, and consommé, and is an interesting alternative to vegetable stocks, especially for vegetarian dishes.
FLAVOUR The aroma is the first sensation you will notice: one of a forest on a damp morning. The flavour is similarly very earthy and fragrant.
STORAGE Store in an airtight container in the fridge up to 1 week, or freeze for up to 1 month.

Basic Recipes

Pasta Dough

MAKES 320G/11OZ

250g/9oz/2 cups pasta flour
5-6 egg yolks

Place the flour and 5 of the yolks in a food processor and mix on high speed for 1 minute. Once it starts to resemble moist breadcrumbs. stop the machine, or add the extra egg yolk if dough appears to be too dry.

Wrap in plastic and put in the fridge to rest for 1 hour before use.

Fish Mousse

MAKES 450G/1LB

150g/5oz trimmed and diced fish such
   as cod, lemon sole or turbot
1 tsp salt
a pinch of ground pepper
300ml/11floz/1¼ cups cream

Place the fish in a food processor and blend to a fine mince, stopping twice during processing to scrape down the sides of the bowl. Add the salt and pepper and mix again ensuring even distribution. Chill for 10-15 minutes.

Place the fish back in the processor then blend in the cream, adding it in a steady stream (this should take only 30-40 seconds otherwise the cream will be overworked and start to separate).

Test-poach a small amount of the mousse by wrapping it in plastic wrap and poaching in simmering water for 1-2 minutes until firm. Taste and adjust the seasoning as necessary. Cover well and store in the fridge for up to 2 days.

This mousse can be made using other fish and seafood however it is necessary to increase the quantity of cream. For salmon use 375ml/13floz/1⅔ cups of cream, for sea bass or monkfish use 500ml/18floz/2¼ cups, and for scallops use 450ml/16floz/2 cups.

Chicken Mousse

MAKES 550G/1LB4OZ

350g/12oz chicken breast fillet, skinned
250ml/9floz/1 cup cream
salt and pepper

Roughly dice the chicken and place in the freezer for 20 minutes to chill.

When the chicken is very cold, place it in a food processor, season with salt and pepper, and process to purée. Add the cream in a steady stream (taking no more than 30-40 seconds otherwise the cream will be overworked).

Test-poach a small amount of the mousse by wrapping it in plastic wrap and poaching in simmering water for 1-2 minutes until firm. Taste and adjust the seasoning as necessary. Store in the fridge for up to 2 days.

Mirepoix

MAKES 1KG/2LB

250g/9oz carrots, peeled
250g/9oz onions, peeled
250g/9oz leeks, trimmed
150g/5oz celery sticks
2 cloves garlic, sliced
1 sprig thyme
½ fresh bay leaf

Cut all the vegetables to the same size, which will vary according to how the mirepoix is to be used. In general, the longer the vegetable is likely to be cooked, the larger the cut. For stock that will be cooking for 12 hours, use the vegetables whole; for braised dishes cut the vegetables into 5cm/2in pieces; for sauces cooking 15-60 minutes cut the vegetables into 2.5cm/1in dice.

Combine the prepared vegetables with the garlic and herbs and use as required in the recipe.

Aubergine Caviar

MAKES 6 HEAPED TBSP

2 medium aubergines (eggplants)
2 cloves garlic, sliced
150ml/5floz/⅔ cup olive oil
2 sprigs thyme
salt and pepper

Heat the oven to 150°C/300°F/Gas 2. Place a large square of kitchen foil on the work surface. Halve the aubergines lengthways and score the flesh in a criss-cross fashion without cutting into the skin.

Place the aubergines on the foil and insert the garlic slices randomly into the cuts. Sprinkle with the oil and thyme sprigs and season with salt and pepper. Cover with another large piece of foil and seal the edges well to make a pouch. Bake for 50 minutes.

Carefully remove the aubergines from the foil. Discard the thyme and leave to cool. Then, using a metal spoon, scrape the flesh from the skin and place in a food processor. Purée for 2-3 minutes until smooth. Taste and adjust the seasoning as necessary. If the mixture is a little wet, place in a pan over medium heat and cook to evaporate the excess liquid. Store chilled for up to 3 days.

Tapenade

MAKES 600G/1LB5OZ

400g/14oz/2⅓ cups pitted black olives
100g/4oz fresh anchovies in vinegar,
 or 50g/2oz brown anchovies in oil
40g/1½oz/2 tbsp capers
2 cloves garlic, peeled
80ml/3floz/⅓ cup olive oil

Place all the ingredients except the olive oil in a food processor and purée for 4-5 minutes. Blend in the oil.

Store in an airtight container in the fridge for up to 3 months.

Garlic Confit

MAKES 12

12 cloves garlic, unpeeled
1 sprig thyme
50ml/2floz/¼ cup olive oil
25g/1oz/2 tbsp sea salt

Heat the oven to 180°C/350°F/Gas 4. Put all the ingredients on a 30cm/12in square of foil and fold to make a parcel, ensuring the edges are well sealed.

Bake for 25 minutes or until the cloves are soft. Remove the garlic from the foil and keep warm until service, or cool and then store in an airtight container for up to 2 days.

Confit Onions

MAKES 24

750g/1lb10oz/3¾ cups duck fat
 or olive oil
24 button onions
1 fresh bay leaf
1 clove garlic, split
1 sprig thyme

Place all the ingredients in a saucepan and heat gently to about 65°C/150°F (warm enough that you can place a finger in it for only 3-4 seconds). Cook for 45-60 minutes or until the onions are tender. Do not allow the fat to get hotter or the onions will start to deep-fry. Store chilled for up to 2 days.

Braised Shallots

MAKES 20

50ml/2floz/¼ cup corn oil
20 medium shallots, peeled, root intact
4 cloves garlic
50g/2oz/½ stick butter
2 sprigs thyme
750ml/1 pint 6floz/3¼ cups chicken
 stock (see page 157)
salt and pepper

Heat the corn oil in a large saucepan. Working in batches if necessary, add the shallots and cook until evenly browned. Add the garlic, butter and thyme cook for another 2 minutes.

Pour in the stock and bring to a boil. Cover and simmer gently for 20-25 minutes or until the shallots are tender. Check regularly to ensure the stock has not evaporated. Season to taste.

Transfer the shallots and their cooking liquid to a container and cool. Cover tightly and store chilled for up to 3 days.

Roasted Onions

MAKES 250G/9OZ

50ml/2floz/¼ cup olive oil
5 large Spanish onions, sliced

Heat the oil in a heavy saucepan and cook the onions over a medium-low heat for 45 minutes ot until the onions are almost dark brown in colour.

Potato Purée

MAKES 6 LARGE SERVINGS

500g/1lb2oz floury potatoes, cubed
250ml/9floz/1 cup double (heavy)
 cream
1 sprig thyme
50g/2oz/½ stick butter
salt and pepper

Place the potatoes in a large saucepan with enough cold salted water to cover. Bring to the boil then lower the heat to just under a simmer and cook for 25-30 minutes until soft.

Meanwhile, boil the cream and thyme in a small saucepan until the volume of liquid has reduced by two-thirds. Pass the cream through a sieve.

Drain the potatoes thoroughly and leave to dry for 10 minutes. Using a masher or ricer, purée the potato. Fold in the cream and butter. Adjust the seasoning as necessary. The purée will keep in the fridge for up to 2 days.

Pumpkin Purée

MAKES 300G/11OZ/1¼ CUP

250g/9oz pumpkin, peeled and
  chopped
25g/1oz/¼ stick butter
salt and pepper

Place the pumpkin in a saucepan and
cover with water. Cover with a tight-
fitting lid, or a piece of greaseproof
paper and the lid, then bring to the
boil and simmer until the pumpkin is
tender. Drain well.

Purée the pumpkin in a food
processor, then mix in the butter and
season to taste. Store in an airtight
container in the fridge for up to 3 days,
or freeze in ice cube trays for 1 month.

Dried Tomato Fillets

MAKES 24

6 plum tomatoes
50ml/2floz/¼ cup olive oil
salt and pepper

Bring a large saucepan of water to the
boil. Meanwhile, prepare an ice bath.
Using a sharp knife, core the tomatoes
and mark a cross in the bases. Place in
the boiling water for 8-10 seconds, then
plunge into the iced water.

Peel the tomatoes, cut lengthways into
quarters and remove the seeds.

Heat the oven to 50°C/130°F/Gas ½.
Lay the tomatoes on a baking tray lined
with foil. Brush with the oil and season
lightly with salt and pepper.

Bake for 2 hours, or until the tomato
fillets shrink to half their original size

and turn deep red. Remove from the
oven and let cool. Store in an airtight
container in the fridge for up to 3 days.

Tomato Concasse

MAKES 250G/9OZ/1 CUP

6 ripe plum tomatoes

Bring a large saucepan of water to the
boil. Meanwhile, prepare an ice bath.
Using a sharp knife, core the tomatoes
and cut a cross in the bases. Plunge them
into the boiling water for 8-10 seconds,
then into the iced water.

Peel the tomatoes, cut lengthways into
quarters and remove the seeds. Put them
on a paper towel and place in the fridge
to dry for 1 hour.

Cut the tomatoes into 5mm/¼in dice,
or whatever size is required. Chill in an
airtight container for up to 1 day.

Chlorophyll

MAKES 2 TBSP

4 litres/3½ pints/4 quarts water
250g/9oz/4½ cups baby spinach leaves
80g/3½oz/4 cups flat parsley leaves
ice cubes

Place the water in a large saucepan and
bring it to 70°C/160°F. Meanwhile, fill
a bowl with ice cubes and set aside. Wash
the leaves and, when the water is ready,
blanch them for 40 seconds.

Using a strainer, transfer the leaves and
3 tbsp of water to a blender. Leave the
pan of water at 70°C/160°F. Liquidize
the leaves on full speed for 6-8 minutes,

checking every 2 minutes and scraping
down the sides of the bowl as necessary,
until you have a bright green liquid.

Discard half the water from the pan.
Add the green liquid to the pan and
stir continuously until there is a distinct
separation of green speckles and water.
Immediately pour the contents of the
pan over the ice in the bowl.

Strain the green liquid through a piece
of muslin, being careful not to force it.
It is best left overnight to drain. The
result should be a green paste resembling
oil paint. Store chilled for up to 2 days.

Herb Oil

MAKES 200ML/7FLOZ/¾ CUP

1 tbsp salt
10g/½oz/½ cup flat parsley leaves
5g/¼oz/¼ cup chives
5g/¼oz/¼ cup basil leaves
100g/4oz baby spinach leaves
250ml/9floz/1 cup corn oil

Heat a large pan of water and add the
salt. Meanwhile, prepare an ice bath to
arrest the cooking. When the water is
boiling, blanch the herbs and spinach
for 2 minutes, then remove immediately
and plunge into the ice bath. Leave
until cold, then drain thoroughly.

Place the blanched herbs in a food
processor with the oil and liquidize at
full power for about 4 minutes or until
the herbs are broken up and the oil has
a distinct herb flavour.

Pour the mixture into an airtight
container and leave to infuse overnight.
Next day, place a clean tea towel or

double layer of muslin over a bowl and secure it with an elastic band or string. Pour the herb mixture onto it and allow the oil to filter into the bowl below. This will take about 2-3 hours but can be left overnight if refrigerated.

Discard the residue in the cloth, being careful not to squeeze through the extra few drops of oil as it may cloud the oil. Decant the flavoured oil into a small jar or bottle for storage and store in the fridge for 3-4 days. Alternatively, it can be frozen.

Mint Oil

MAKES 150ML/5FLOZ/²⁄₃ CUP

1 tbsp salt
20g/¾oz/1 cup packed mint leaves
150ml/5floz/²⁄₃ cup corn oil

Heat a large pan of water and add the salt. Meanwhile, prepare an ice bath to arrest the cooking. When the water is boiling, blanch the mint for 1 minute, then remove immediately and plunge into the ice bath. Leave until cold, then drain thoroughly.

Place the blanched mint in a food processor with the oil and liquidize at full power for about 4 minutes or until the herbs are broken up and the oil has a distinct mint flavour. Pour the mixture into an airtight container and leave to infuse overnight.

Next day, place a clean tea towel or double layer of muslin over a bowl and secure it with an elastic band or string. Pour the mint mixture onto it and allow the oil to filter into the bowl

below. This will take about 2-3 hours but can be left overnight if refrigerated.

Discard the residue in the cloth, being careful not to squeeze through the extra few drops of oil as it may cloud the oil. Decant the oil into a small jar or bottle for storage and store in the fridge for 3-4 days. Alternatively, it can be frozen in ice cube trays.

Basil Oil

MAKES 200ML/7FLOZ/¾ CUP

10g/½oz/½ cup flat parsley leaves
10g/½oz/½ cup basil leaves
250ml/9floz/1 cup corn oil

Heat a large pan of water. Meanwhile, prepare an ice bath to arrest the cooking of the herbs. Blanch the herbs for 2½ minutes, then remove immediately and plunge into the ice bath. Leave until cold, then drain thoroughly.

Place the blanched herbs in a food processor with the oil and liquidize at full power for about 4 minutes or until the herbs are broken up and the oil has a strong basil flavour. Pour the mixture into an airtight container and leave to infuse overnight.

Next day, place a clean tea towel or double layer of muslin over a bowl and secure it with an elastic band or string. Pour the herb mixture onto it and allow the oil to filter into the bowl below. This will take about 2-3 hours but can be left overnight if refrigerated.

Discard the residue in the cloth, being careful not to squeeze through the extra few drops of oil as it may

cloud the oil. Decant the oil into a jar and store in the fridge for 3-4 days. Alternatively, freeze in ice cube trays.

Lemon Oil

MAKES 250ML/9FLOZ/1 CUP

pared rind of 3 lemons, pith removed
1 stalk lemongrass, halved lengthways
    and cut into 2.5cm/1in pieces
250ml/9floz/1 cup grapeseed oil
2 tbsp olive oil

Place all the ingredients in a food processor and pulse until the rind and lemongrass are 3mm/⅛in thick.

Transfer to a jar and leave to stand for 2 days at room temperature. Decant and store the clear oil in the fridge or freezer for up to 2 months, however the flavour will gradually dissipate.

Basic Vinaigrette

MAKES 250ML/9FLOZ/1 CUP

50ml/2floz/¼ cup grapeseed or corn oil
25ml/1floz/2 tbsp sherry vinegar
1 tsp wholegrain mustard
125ml/4floz/½ cup light olive oil
salt and pepper

Place the grapeseed or corn oil in a large bowl with the vinegar and mustard and whisk to an emulsion. Slowly add the olive oil 4 tbsp at a time, whisking to re-emulsify after each addition, then season to taste with salt and pepper.

Pour into a jar or bottle and store in the fridge until ready to use. If the dressing separates, shake to re-emulsify.

Strawberry Dressing

MAKES APPROX 250ML/9FLOZ/1 CUP

70ml/3floz/⅓ cup white wine vinegar
120ml/4floz/½ cup corn oil
50ml/2floz/¼ cup olive oil
30g/1oz/2 tbsp whole grain mustard
70g/2¼oz/½ cup strawberries, hulled

Place all the ingredients in a food processor and purée until emulsified. Pour the dressing into a jar, then cover and chill for up to 3 days.

Truffle Dressing

MAKES 200ML/7FLOZ/¾ CUP

1 egg yolk
1 tsp balsamic vinegar
1 tsp sherry vinegar
½ tsp chopped truffle (optional)
50ml/2floz/¼ cup olive oil
50ml/2floz/¼ cup corn or grapeseed oil
4 tsp truffle oil
salt and pepper

Place the yolk in a mixing bowl with both vinegars and the chopped truffle, if using. Whisk until a whitish foam appears, then slowly add all the oils.

Season to taste and store in a plastic airtight container for up to 2 days.

Red Wine Jus

MAKES 250ML/9FLOZ/1 CUP

50ml/2floz/¼ cup corn oil
2 carrots, cut into 2.5/1in cubes
1 stick celery, cut into 2.5/1in cubes
1 leek, cut into 2.5/1in cubes
1 large shallot, cut into 2.5/1in cubes

1 Bramley apple, cored but not peeled and cut into 1cm/½in dice
200ml/7floz/scant 1 cup red wine
150ml/5floz/⅔ cup apple juice
1.2 litres/2 pints/1 quart lamb jus (see page 156)
1 clove garlic, split
2 sprigs thyme
salt and pepper
sugar, to taste

Heat the oil in a heavy saucepan and sauté the vegetables, not the apple, for 6-7 minutes or until light golden brown. Add the apple and cook for 2 minutes.

Pour the red wine and apple juice into the pan and scrape up any sediment from the bottom using a wooden spoon. Bring to the boil and simmer until reduced by half.

Add the lamb jus, garlic and thyme. Bring to a slow simmer and cook for 20 minutes. Pass through a fine sieve, season to taste and, if the mixture is a little bitter, add some sugar.

Leave to cool, partially covered by plastic film to ensure the steam escapes. Once cool, cover tightly and place in the fridge for up to 1 week. The jus will set and needs to be brought back to warm room temperature to serve.

Duck Spice

SERVES 8

1 tbsp five-spice powder
2 star anise
½ tsp ground cumin
8 cloves
½ tsp black peppercorns

Place all the ingredients in a dry pan and heat gently over a low heat, stirring frequently, until fragrant.

Grind to a fine powder and store in an airtight container for up to 3 days. The spice mixture can be frozen but the flavour dissipates over time.

Tempura Batter

MAKES 400G/14OZ

100g/3½oz/¾ cup plain flour
100g/3½oz/¾ cup cornflour (cornstarch)
200ml/7floz/1 scant cup sparkling mineral or soda water (seltzer)
salt and pepper

Place all the ingredients in a mixing bowl and whisk to a smooth batter. Use within 1 hour.

Puff Pastry

MAKES 1.25KG/2LB12OZ

500g/1lb2oz/4 cups plain flour
500g/1lb2oz/4½ sticks butter, cut into 5cm/2in cubes
4 tsp salt
250ml/9floz/about 1 cup ice-cold water

Place the flour, butter and salt in the bowl of an electric mixer and mix on slow speed until the butter has reduced to 2.5cm/1in cubes, about 1-2 minutes. Slowly add the water to form a dough.

Place the dough on a clean, floured work surface. Roll the dough away from you into a rectangle measuring 25.5 x 13cm/10 x 5in. Bring the top edge of the dough back towards you, placing the end two-thirds of the way down the strip. Fold the bottom edge up over this, then turn the pastry square over and repeat the rolling and folding process. Cover and chill for 20 minutes.

Roll and fold the pastry again, then leave to rest for 20 minutes before use. Store for up to 3 days in the fridge or up to 2 weeks in the freezer.

Savoury Tuile

MAKES 20

150g/5oz/1¼ cups icing (confectioners') sugar
60g/2oz/⅓ cup plain flour
60g/2oz/½ stick butter, melted
2 tbsp chlorophyll (see page 161)
salt and pepper

Place all the ingredients in a bowl and beat to a smooth paste. Rest in the fridge for 1 hour, or store for up to 5 days.

Heat the oven to 180C/350°F/Gas 4. Line a baking sheet with nonstick parchment and spread thinly with the tuile mixture. Bake for 6-8 minutes until the tuiles are translucent.

Cool, remove carefully and store in an airtight container for 1 day.

Fruit Tuile

MAKES 30

200g/7oz/2 cups icing (confectioners') sugar
50g/2oz/½ cup plain flour
100g/4oz/1 cup berry coulis (see right) or other fruit purée
80g/3oz/¾ stick melted butter

Place all the ingredients in a bowl and beat to a smooth paste. Chill for 1 hour or store in the fridge for up to 5 days.

Heat the oven to 180°C/350°F/Gas 4. Line a baking sheet with nonstick parchment and spread thinly with the tuile mixture. Bake for 6-8 minutes until translucent. Cool, remove carefully and store in an airtight container for 1 day.

Brandy Snap

MAKES 20

120g/4½oz/⅔ cup sugar
110g/4oz/⅓ cup golden (corn) syrup
70g/2¾oz/¾ stick butter
110g/4oz/¾ cup plain flour, sifted

Place the sugar, syrup and butter in a saucepan and bring to the boil. Slowly mix in the flour. Remove from the heat, transfer to an airtight container and chill for 2 hours, or up to 1 week.

Heat the oven to 180C/350°F/Gas 4. Line a baking sheet with nonstick parchment. Roll the mixture into balls of the desired size (peanut for small, grape for large) and place on the baking sheet at 15cm/6in intervals.

Bake for 8-10 minutes until golden brown. Allow to cool slightly on the tray before removing. Store in an airtight container for up to 2 weeks.

Berry Coulis

MAKES 400G/14OZ/1¾ CUPS

225g/8oz/2 cups fresh red berries
225g/8oz/2 cups icing (confectioners') sugar

Place the berries and sugar in bowl and leave to macerate for 20 minutes. When the berries have started to bleed, place them and the juice into a food processor and purée. Pass through fine sieve. Store chilled for up to 3 days.

Stock Syrup

MAKES 750ML/1 PINT 6FLOZ/4¼ CUPS

500ml/18floz/2¼ cups water
250g/9oz/1¼ cups sugar

Place the water and sugar in a large saucepan and heat until the sugar is completely dissolved. Store chilled for up to 1 week. This is for hard fruits such as pears and apples. For soft fruits such as berries and apricots, increase the sugar to 500g/1lb2oz/2½ cups.

Crème Pâtissière

MAKES 600G/1LB 5OZ

500ml/18floz/2¼ cups semi-skimmed milk
100g/4oz/⅔ cup sugar
50g/2oz/½ cup cornflour (cornstarch)
3 eggs

Place 400ml/14floz/1¾ cups of the milk in a saucepan and bring to scalding point. Meanwhile, in a large bowl, mix the remaining milk with the sugar, cornflour and eggs.

Pour the scalding milk onto the egg mixture and stir well. Return to a clean pan and cook, stirring continuously, until thick. Cool, then store in an airtight container in the fridge for up to 3 days.

Science and Methodology

No cookbook can highlight every way in which a recipe can potentially go wrong as there is a human element involved. Understanding the basic nature of food and its cooking methods puts you in a good position to correct any mistakes and create a more spontaneous, free-flowing style of working in the kitchen. It will also free you from the need to always follow directions word for word. This section explains the science and methodology behind several of this book's dishes.

Water Hardness

Pure water has a Ph level of 7.0, but water is rarely pure. Even rain water and distilled water contain some dissolved materials.

Hard water can cause difficulties when cooking pulses since the magnesium and calcium in the water interfere with tenderising these foods. Likewise, an acidic cooking medium will prevent dried beans absorbing water and softening properly.

This also applies to bread making but not with disastrous results. The quality of the finished product is just as good but when made with a soft water the dough tends to be more lively, whereas hard water will retard the dough slightly.

When cooking green vegetables in hard water, the cell walls and pectin become more soluble than in soft water and thus the vegetable's colour is lost more rapidly. However it also means the chlorophyll can be easily removed (see Cooking Green Vegetables overleaf for more on chlorophyll extraction).

Egg Cookery

When cooking eggs or egg dishes it is important not to prolong the cooking. Eventually the proteins will stiffen and squeeze out the liquid, rendering the egg or egg dish rubbery, less tender and not very appetising.

When poaching whole eggs, using a dilute acidic cooking medium (5-7 per cent vinegar in the water) will help retain the egg's shape by speeding up the coagulation. Make sure the water is close to – not at – boiling point as turbulent water will break down the outer albumen of the egg and cause the yolk and white to separate.

Take particular care when making custards. The safety margin before the mixture splits is very small. Therefore, as the custard starts to coagulate at 78-82°C/172-179°F, it must be passed through a fine sieve into a clean bowl that you have set in ice or a sink of cold water, otherwise the residual heat will cause the custard to separate, scrambling the eggs.

Egg whites make excellent foams as they can be increased by as much as eight times their original volume by whisking. However, this will be inhibited by as much as two-thirds if even a tiny amount of egg yolk is left in the whites. It is the fat molecules in the egg yolk that causes this reaction; other fats and oils are not as disastrous but can inhibit the whites to such an extent that plastic bowls should be avoided. The chemical compound of plastic is similar to that which forms the bulk of all fat molecules, therefore attracting traces of fat on the surface which will in turn retard the aeration. Stainless steel and copper bowls are the preferred choice.

Whipping and Whisking

The terms soft and stiff peak are associated with whisking cream and egg whites. When cream is whipped, air is knocked into the fat molecules. The more you whip, the more air goes in until eventually the fat molecules are saturated with air and the liquid content of the cream is squeezed out.

When a recipe requires semi-whipped or softly whipped cream, it should just hold its own weight in the bowl, especially when further mixing is required, as when making a mousse.

Sponge and other cakes normally require egg whites to be whisked to a soft peak while meringue or soufflés require a stiff peak. As the sponge has other aerating properties, too much rise from the eggs will give an over-aerated product with very little structure once removed from the oven.

In soufflés and meringues the whisked egg whites are the only raising agent so it is necessary to introduce as much air as possible into the protein molecules. Once heated, they expand to give a good lift.

Soufflé Making

As long as you follow the key principles of soufflé making, you should be able to make soufflés successfully from whatever flavourings you prefer without using a recipe.

When whipping the egg whites, the bowl and whisk must be free from fat or grease. Indeed, you should avoid all fats when making soufflés as they inhibit the egg proteins and burst the air bubbles. The egg whites and sugar should be whisked to a smooth, stiff peak with small air bubbles – the smaller the air bubbles, the bigger the lift. The purée used to flavour the soufflé should be reasonably thick as this will help to support the soufflé while cooking.

The mould must be well-greased to ensure the proteins in the egg do not stick to the glaze on the porcelain. Make sure you clean off any excess soufflé mixture from around the rim of the dish as this could cause the soufflé to stick and prevent it rising evenly. And remember always to put the unbaked soufflé into a hot oven.

Mousse Making

The principles of savoury mousse making are simple but must be followed accurately to ensure a perfect result. Firstly, the prepared meat or fish must be free of all sinew and gristle as these fibres will not break down and will give a grainy result. Salt also plays a big role. It causes the protein in the meat or fish to swell, firming up the flesh and aiding the incorporation of cream.

The temperature of the mixture while it is being worked in the food processor is also crucial. A prolonged mixing process creates heat and if cold cream is added to a tepid mixture, the liquids, fats and solids will separate, giving a grainy texture. A useful hint is to add the cream in a steady stream but fairly quickly otherwise the cream will separate.

Risotto Making

In general, most restaurants do not serve risotto, they serve a bastardised version of it. They cook the risotto well before service and keep it in the fridge for 6-8 hours. The reason is that it would be logistically impossible to serve traditionally made risotto in a busy restaurant.

The method I have given is the way I cook risotto both at the restaurant and at home. Personally, in my view, there is very little difference to the end result (sorry risotto gurus) and my method is easier for the cook to serve.

There are several key steps to good risotto. Ensure your stock is of good quality and at a simmer. Make sure you stir and nurture the rice constantly during cooking. Balance the ratio of stock to butter when finishing the dish to give a good emulsion (this is perhaps the most important part of making a top-quality risotto). Adjust the seasoning towards the end of cooking as the gradually reducing stock will steadily increase the dish's flavour during the cooking process. As long as you observe these fundamental principles, you should be able to develop an excellent risotto from any ingredients you choose.

Meat Cookery

Here is a test for doneness when cook meat that should not be applied as a blanket rule, but certainly helps when you are less than confident or do not cook meat on a regular basis.

First, open the hand you do not write with, palm facing towards you. Using the little finger of that hand, and applying only a little pressure, touch the tip of the thumb. Keep the hand in that position and, with the index finger of the other hand, touch the mound of fleshy muscle beneath the thumb of your non-writing hand – this feeling is what you should look for when you require meat well done.

Next place the ring finger of your weakest hand on the tip of the thumb and again touch the muscle under the thumb with the index finger of your strong hand – this is the sensation of medium-well done meat. Follow this technique through each finger to see if meat is cooked to the degree you require. Use the middle finger for medium meat, and the forefinger for rare-medium. The system needs to be altered slightly for new season lamb, in that the middle finger will indicate medium-well done meat and the forefinger will indicate medium.

When fibrous proteins are heated they contract and this squeezes out the liquid. For example, when a steak is cooked the proteins contract, squeezing out all the water or juices. If the heat is increased or continues, the steak will then become dry and the eating quality will be impaired.

Cuts of meat also contain elastin and collagen. Elastin (associated with tendons and arteries) is extremely stretchy and further cooking adds to its strength. Collagen (the main muscle proteins that are the greatest part of the muscle) is tough and chewy. Meat that has a high proportion of both, usually from the highly worked muscle groups, is not suitable for quick cooking such as grilling. However if these cuts of meat are cooked in liquid for a long period at the correct temperature (braising), the collagen will dissolve in the water, forming gelatine and producing a tasty joint.

Prime cuts such as beef fillet have little collagen in their makeup and do not require long cooking to tenderize the meat. Although most chefs use a high temperature for a short period on these cuts, it does not always yield a perfect result. Due to the lack of fat and collagen, high heat renders the muscle fibers dry and consequently the eating quality is impaired. A lower temperature and longer period in the oven produces a gradual heat, therefore there is less extreme coagulation in the tissues, and less fluid is squeezed out.

Traditionally a fillet steak, for example, would be sealed in hot oil (180-200°C/350-375°F) and then the heat would be reduced slightly to finish the cooking. The process that takes place is one of thermal energy or molecular conduction: the first layer of molecules heats the next and so on until the desired degree of cooking is achieved at the core of the steak. To achieve a core temperature of 55-60°C/131-140°F, 25 per cent of the meat would be overcooked. Therefore if the meat is sealed in hot oil for 20-30 seconds, removed and placed in the oven at a reduced temperature of 59°C/138°F (just before the protein collapses) and cooked for a longer period, through molecular conduction more than 95 per cent of the meat will be perfectly cooked. An example of this is the slow-cooked beef with onion ice cream (see page 88).

Please note that the above temperatures are for beef and are not appropriate for poultry or pork.

Fish Cookery

The freshness of any ingredient is important, but when it comes to fish and shellfish it is absolutely paramount due to the short shelf life of the product. Because of this brief time in which to sell the freshest fish, poor or sub-standard quality is often sold, so avoid the cheap deals. When sourcing a good fishmonger, choose one that has a high standard of hygiene in the shop and not a foul fish smell that lingers.

When choosing fresh fish, there are a few key signs to look for. Funnily enough it should not smell fishy, but should smell of the sea. The gills should be red and not grey, the eyes should be clear, not cloudy or dry, and the skin should be smooth and moist, not slimy or dehydrated.

Care should be taken when cooking as fish has little (about 3 per cent in some cases) or no connective tissue, which gives it a flaky texture and makes it prone to drying out. A low temperature and long cooking time can be used to ensure a delicately finished product. When cooking the mi-cuit salmon dish (see page 60), the temperature is very important. The protein in most fish starts to toughen at 41°C/105°F. If the cooking process is set under that point, at 40°C/102°F, the fish will be cooked through but not tough and the flesh will have become opaque.

This temperature may seem a little low, but if a good organic or wild salmon is cooked in a little oil at a high temperature until all the flesh is pink, as opposed to orange, the finished dish will taste powdery and dry – a great shame and a waste of a fine ingredient. The general rule is to use a little oil and seal the fish on one side quickly to give a crisp skin, then turn it over, add a little butter, reduce the heat right down and cook slowly until there is a thin opaque line through the centre. This method will yield a fair compromise between a roasted flavour, crisp skin and tender flesh.

Cooking Green Vegetables

The application of heat, whether it is by boiling, baking or stir-frying, will tenderize vegetables by weakening the cell walls and extracting water from the plant cell. The problem one faces when cooking vegetables is to not overcook them. Usually we take the common sense approach by sampling the vegetable while it is cooking and stopping the process when the vegetable is tender but still firm.

The one principle you must pay heed to when cooking green vegetables is the temperature. The danger zone, as it were, is when the green pigmentation (chlorophyll) bleeds from the plant cells at 66-77°C/150-170°F. The skill is to reduce the time they are exposed to this danger zone. Putting green vegetables into boiling water forces them to pass through this zone as quickly as possible on the way up. Once cooked, immersing them immediately in an ice bath forces them to pass quickly through this zone while cooling.

Stock Making

For some chefs, stocks are quite personal and they may have a different approach or method from others. The methods of stock making I use are unusual in that the time and temperature differ from the norm, but they work for me and my food style. The classical theory remains paramount and the reasons for my basic principles are as follows.

Keeping the vegetables whole gives a smaller surface area to volume ratio and thus reduces the likelihood of the vegetables breaking down to form a soupy consistency.

Cooking the stock on a very low temperature (candle light) draws out the flavours slowly, like an infusion, as opposed to the aggressive extraction of boiling that would yield various indifferent results, including a bitter, dry aftertaste, poor or soapy flavour, and a cloudy finish.

Roasting the bones at a precise temperature prevents a bitter flavour in the stock. The flavour we associate with browned meat comes from a very complex chemical reaction called the Maillard reaction, which is the browning effect on all foods when heat is applied. This takes place at 140-175°C/275-347°F. The chemical reaction that takes place predominantly concerns the sugars in the meat, which turn from caramelization to a burnt state at 176°C/349°F. Therefore it is important to avoid temperatures above 175°C/347°F when roasting bones for stock, otherwise the stock will taste bitter and harsh.

Sauce Foams

These are a key example of the less-volume-more-taste element of my cooking. Sauce foams comprise an intense stock that has been reduced to a syrupy consistency, with milk added and brought to a foam as for a cappuccino. They can be made easily at home without an espresso machine. The most important factor is that the milk mixture should not be brought to a boil as boiled milk cannot be agitated to a foam.

To produce your own, simply make a mixture of 20 per cent reduced stock or essence, 75 per cent milk and 5 per cent butter. Heat it to approximately 80°C/176°F and whisk the milk until a foam appears. Allow it to settle for 30 seconds, then spoon off the flavoured bubbles.

Seasoning

Seasoning is the ability to heighten or draw out the essential flavours in a specific foodstuff by using condiments. There many ways of seasoning a dish. The most common are salt and pepper but others include acid (in the form of citrus or vinegar), sugar, herbs, spices and powders. The art is to bring the flavour of the main ingredient to the forefront but not so much that you taste the seasoning itself. The condiment should be a foundation of the dish, supporting not protruding. Generally, if you can taste salt in a dish it is too salty.

Salting

Food has been salted for thousands of years with the principal aim being to rid the product of harmful microbes to extend the shelf life. This was particularly advantageous before refrigeration. Salt also extracts moisture through osmosis rendering the salted ingredient firm.

This technique is used on the cod for the chowder (see page 15) for a similar reason. Due to the lack of connective tissue in the fish's flesh, drawing out a little moisture from the surface will reduce the flaky properties of the cod.

Drying

Drying is a form of preservation, however another primary purpose of the drying process is to extract moisture from the food and therefore intensify its flavour. This suits my aim to reduce the volume of food served while intensifying its flavour in order to create a pleasurable dining experience. Powders, such as those made from mushrooms (see page 96) or raspberries (see page 128) are one means of offering an intense boost of flavour with little volume.

Composing your own dishes

There are so many variables in dish composition – flavour and texture balance, presentation, portion size, what will be served before and after, time of day... the list could be endless. As the cook or chef, you must first determine the aim or purpose of any dish you produce. It is the reference point from which you can start cooking and creating. Here are a few tips to help you through this culinary minefield.

FLAVOUR EXTRACTION The primary factor influencing my dishes is flavour. The food may look fantastic and the ingredients may be at their peak, but if the dish has no flavour the moment is lost. One of the greatest puzzles a chef faces is how to coax as much flavour from an ingredient as possible; it is like the Holy Grail! You must either isolate the flavours or encourage them by pairing them with other ingredients, flavours or taste sensations. You might, for example, add a touch of salt to a sweet preparation, or a little sherry vinegar to a rich sauce. Both of these are good flavour enhancers. My advice is to be patient: experiment with seasoning by adding-tasting, adding-tasting, and with time you will understand how flavours work and how to bring out the best in your food.

BALANCE OF FLAVOURS Balance is often ignored, even by some professionals, but underpins the foundation of flavour upon which the whole dish is based. You need to offer enough variety of flavour and texture to avoid boring the palate, while at the same time not allowing one taste or texture to dominate and ensuring that all of the flavours are harmonious. Again this is something you will develop with time and patience, but basic errors include making all aspects of a dish creamy or soft, or all crunchy, and not including a range of tastes such as sweet, savoury, acid and salty.

PORTION SIZE This, too, is crucial. If the dish is too big it will spoil the next course and probably the rest of the meal. Remember your dish's focus, the reference point from which you started. Keeping this in mind will help you assess how large or small each course should be. In my view it is best to offer many small courses rather than two or three larger ones.

The reason is that, after a few mouthfuls, the taste receptors become accustomed to the dish. Therefore serving several smaller portions heightens your guests' dining experience, which is why tasting menus are such fun to eat.

CONTROL When designing or composing a dish, a key skill is knowing when to stop adding ingredients. A good chef will stop just at the right time, ignoring inessentials and allowing the true essence of the dish to be at the forefront. An over-eager chef will spoil the dish by overcrowding it with flavours and textures, trying to impress. Less is certainly more, and if the fundamental combination works and the ingredients are at their best, it is hard to go wrong. Exercise control – know when to stop.

PRESENTATION When I cook at the restaurant I have a brigade of chefs working with me to produce a number of meals for any one service. When cooking at home you will not have this support. In the restaurant we can spend time on food presentation as we have the facilities to do so without compromising the flavour or composition of the finished dish. We also need to maintain an accurate standard for which guests are happy to pay. The dishes need to look and taste the same day in and day out; having no set standard of presentation would open the door to creative chaos, or inconsistency at the very least. However, when I cook at home I almost never use elaborate presentation. Home cooks need to strike a balance between the dish's composition, flavour and presentation, but put the ultimate emphasis on taste. Always try to understand your resources at home and work within their limitations.

Glossary

BAKING BEANS Used to weigh down pastry when pre-baking in a tart case or mould to prevent it raising or bubbling. You can buy ready made baking weights/beans but these can be quite expensive. A cheap alternative is to use dried peas or beans.

BLANCH To dip a food into boiling water briefly, then refresh it in cold water. It may be used to prepare food for peeling, part-cooking or freezing.

BEIGNET A sweet or savoury food, rolled in flour, then in a light batter and deep fried. Direct translation: fritter

BRAISE A cooking method that involves browning meat (usually a tough fibrous cut high in collagen such as shin, shoulder, skirt, topside), then adding stock and flavourings and cooking until tender in a covered container to inhibit evaporation. The method can also be applied to vegetables, in which case they would normally be cooked with no or very little browning, but still in a well flavoured liquid in a covered container.

CARAMELIZATION To cook to a rich golden colour giving a glazed effect to the food.

CONFIT Traditionally this term indicated the slow cooking of duck or goose (usually leg) in its own fat. The word is now used very loosely by chefs, however it tends to mean food cooked slowly in oil or fat, or food cooked in its own fat or juices.

COULIS A smooth purée with a thick sauce consistency made predominately with fruit, sometimes with sugar added.

CRACKED PEPPER Whole peppercorns that have been cracked with a mortar and pestle, or between a pan and chopping board. It is not as fine as milled or freshly ground pepper.

DECANT To pour a liquid from one container to another without disturbing the sediment that has settled at the bottom of the first container. The term is commonly used in relation to serving fine red wines however in this book it is applied to infused lemon oil, where the clear flavoured oil is poured away from the flavouring ingredients before storage or serving.

DEGLAZE To add stock, alcohol or water to a pan in which food (especially meat or poultry) has been cooked and swirl it around to remove the sediment or caramelized cooking juices from the base of the pan, usually while stirring vigorously with a wooden spoon.

EMULSION The result of combining two liquids that would not usually mix, such as dispersing fats in a watery liquid. It is achieved by agitating one whilst adding the other. Mayonnaise is an emulsion, so is risotto. When making risotto, the emulsion is formed by stirring the stock and butter together to form a smooth mass that clings to the rice in the pan, thus creating a single mass of rice.

FOLD Incorporating two or more ingredients or mixtures without the expulsion of air, normally using a whisk, large spoon or spatula. Typically used in making soufflés and mousses.

FONDANT Directly translated as 'melt in the mouth'. The term can be associated with vegetable dishes, such as carrot or potato fondant, or with desserts, such as chocolate fondant. It is a description rather than a method.

FONDU There are many uses of this term. Most common is in reference to a pot of warm liquid, such as cheese or chocolate, placed in the centre of the table with pieces of food for dipping. In this book fondu is associated with a vegetable preparation of tomatoes cut into fine dice and cooked over a low heat in butter until soft.

GLACÉ A heavily reduced stock in the form of a syrup.

GLUCOSE SYRUP A clear thick, viscous inverted syrup used in sweet preparations to prevent recrystallisation, particularly of boiled sugar. It is also used in some ice creams as it lowers the freezing temperature of the mixture and retards the formation of ice crystals but gives less sweetness than sugar.

ICE BATH A container filled with two parts water and one part ice, used to arrest the cooking process, especially when blanching vegetables and making egg dishes such as custards.

INFUSE Steeping an aromatic substance in liquid until the liquid has absorbed the desired degree of flavour.

JUS A French term, the translation of which is 'juice'. It would traditionally be used to describe a meat gravy extracted from the pan after cooking by deglazing, then reducing to a slightly thicker sauce that would be passed through a sieve and served. It could also refer to a direct extraction of juice from a raw fruit or vegetable. Today, however, the term jus often indicates the reduction of stock, usually lamb or a similar dark stock, to a fine viscous consistency with an intense flavour. It is used very sparingly and once chilled, sets hard. Jus in this jellied form can be reconstituted to make stock.

NAGE A lightly flavoured, clear stock, usually made from mushrooms and vegetables, similar to a broth. Nages are highly versatile and could be used in soups, risottos and sauces when a strong flavour is not required.

PASS The process of pouring a liquid through a medium or fine strainer to remove lumps, sediment and flavourings such as herbs, spices and mirepoix. Passing is also used in opposite fashion to remove excess moisture from purées, in which case the solids are kept and the liquid usually discarded.

PURÉE A thick, smooth substance made from fruit or vegetables, raw or cooked. Purées can be made in several ways, including liquidizing the food in a food processor, passing it through a fine sieve, a combination of these, or using a food mill or mouli-legumes. The term purée can also be a verb, in which case it refers to the action of making the food thick and smooth.

QUENELLE The direct translation is 'oval shape'. A quenelle is made by using two spoons, small or large, in a rolling action to shape mixtures into an oval. It can be used for most mixtures of firm consistency (see page 57).

REDUCE Vigorously boiling a liquid in an uncovered pan so that the liquid evaporates, thickens slightly, and intensifies in flavour.

REFRESH To plunge just-cooked vegetables into ice-cold water to stop the cooking process quickly and prevent loss of colour in the vegetables.

RESIDUAL HEAT The heat that remains in a pan of food once it has been removed from the heat source. It can cause secondary or further cooking in certain recipes. Care should be taken when the success of a dish demands a narrow margin of temperature, such as fish and egg cookery, especially custard.

SABAYON Traditionally refers to an aerated sweet sauce made by whisking egg yolks with sugar and alcohol. The term now also indicates an egg yolk mixture of similar consistency, sometimes made with the application of heat.

SILPAT A nonstick baking mat made from a rubber compound that can withstand high temperatures. It is ideal for cooking pastry products, or fragile or thinly sliced ingredients when drying them to a crisp.

SWEAT The slow cooking (usually of vegetables) in oil or fat to extract their flavour without adding colour.

WILTED A cooking method usually associated with green leafy vegetables of a high water content such as chard, spinach and lettuce. They are placed in a hot dry pan with a little butter and seasoning, cooked for a brief period then removed and served immediately.

Notes on the recipes

The names and types of ingredients expressed in brackets are for the benefit of American and Australasian readers who have a different cookery language from Britain and are not always able to buy the same products. Australasian readers please note that this book features 8floz imperial cup measurements and 15ml tablespoons (equal to 3 teaspoons). The pint measures given are British and equivalent to 20floz; Americans should use the cup measures provided instead. Readers can use any type of measurement they feel comfortable with, however it is important not to switch between units of measurement while cooking as the quantities given are not exact conversions, nor should they be. The purpose of conversions is to allow people to easily use their preferred units of measurement, not to present them with an exact translation of grams to ounces and cups.

Other important points to note when using this book:

- Eggs are free range and large unless otherwise stated. Americans should use extra large eggs.
- All butter used in the recipes is unsalted.
- Cream is whipping cream unless otherwise stated. Americans should use heavy whipping cream.
- Sugar is caster sugar unless otherwise stated. Americans should use granulated sugar except on occasions where confectioners' sugar is specifically stated.
- Where a recipe specifies plain flour, Americans should use all-purpose flour.
- Chocolate is 70 per cent cocoa solids content unless otherwise stated.

- Gelatine is bronze leaf.
- Spoon measures are level unless otherwise stated.
- Oven temperatures and times are variable depending on equipment; some adjustment of temperature or timing may be needed.
- Portion sizes are suitable for a three course meal but may be reduced to suit a larger or tasting menu.
- If time necessitates using bought stock, do so sparingly as commercially produced stocks tend to have a high salt content.
- If you substitute dried herbs for fresh add only half the amount.
- Read through the recipe at least once to familiarize yourself with all the components before you make it.

Index

Suppliers and Sources

Meat

Fairfax Meadow
24/27 Regis Road, Kentish Town,
London NW5 3EZ.
Tel: 020 7428 3800
My butcher

Chesterton Farm
Butchers Shop, Chesterton Lane,
Cirencester, Glouscestershire GL7 6JP.
Tel: 01285 642160
Specialty breeds

For a list of quality butchers in your
area please contact:
Q Guild of Butchers
Tel: 01383 432608

Fish

Tim Alsop
The Loft Office, The Fish Market,
Buller Quay, East Looe PL13 1DX.
Tel: 01503 240226
My fishmonger

Island Divers
Rose Cottage, Reraig, Balmacara,
Ross Shire, Scotland IV40 8DH.
Tel: 01599 566 248
Shellfish

For a list of quality fishmongers in your
area please contact:
The National Federation of
Fishmongers
Tel: 01376 571391

Herbs and Mushrooms

Halcyon Herbs
14 Modena Road, Hove, East Sussex
BN3 5QG.
Tel: 01273 721049
Specialty salad leaves and seeds

Wild Harvest
31 London Stone Business Estate,
Broughton Street, London SW1 3QJ.
Tel: 020 7498 5397
Wild mushrooms

Specialty Ingredients

Grivan Products
New Covent Garden Market,
Nine Elms Lane, London SW8 5LL.
Tel: 020 7627 9666
Speciality goods, foie gras, vanilla etc

Equipment

Villeroy & Boch Tableware
267 Merton Road, London SW18 5JS.
Tel: 020 8871 0011
Crockery and tableware

Russums Mail Order
Edward House, Tenter Street,
Rotherham, South Yorkshire S60 1LB.
Tel: 01709 372345
Specialist catering supplies

For more on John Campbell visit
www.chefcampbell.com

Acknowledgements

Few people manage success alone:

Jenni Muir, my editor, the catalyst for this book; for her
meticulous attention to detail and encouragement in meeting
deadlines. Iain Shelton and Empire Ventures for their support
over the past four years. Heston Blumenthal, for his true
inspiration and passionate conversation, a true culinary genius.
The team at the Lords of the Manor, past and present, for
their relentless support and guidance. Nathan Outlaw, my sous
chef and good friend, whose loyalty and dedication over the
past two years have helped shape the current brigade.
Professor David Foskett, Maureen Mills, Tim Alsop, Jerry, Rob
and James for believing in me many years ago. Chris Galvin, a
true chef. The extraordinary team at Conran Octopus,
designer Carl Hodson and photographer Sam Bailey.

A special thank you must also go to Richard Young and
Elizabeth Carter, for their passions and character as well their
capacity to express and teach true hospitality. For this and
their ability to be honest, I am truly grateful.

Thank you.